THE GOSPEL ACCORDING TO ST. MARK

Sermons by
The Revd. KARL A. PRZYWALA

C&P
C & P Books

Copyright © 2018 Karl A. Przywala

All rights reserved. No part of this book may be used or reproduced by any means, graphic, electronic, or mechanical, including photocopying, recording, taping or by any information storage retrieval system without the written permission of the author, except in the case of brief quotations embodied in academic discussions, critical articles and reviews.

ISBN: 978-1-7751062-5-8 (sc)
ISBN: 978-1-7751062-6-5 (e)

C&P Books third printing 12/20/2019

To those who have gone before me

and those who will follow

FOREWORD

The Revd. Karl Przywala's engaging volume is especially valuable in being a collection of sermons that move sequentially through every chapter of Mark, thus allowing the reader to fit carefully explained details into the ongoing sweep of the narrative.

These sermons, which were delivered at Holy Trinity Anglican Church in Vancouver, BC between March 2014 and April 2016, are written in a clear, graceful style; they are sparked with humour and attention-getting points and are designed to encourage people in their Christian lives by applying Mark's words to their personal situations.

Karl has a remarkable ability to make complex ideas understandable without watering down the material. He combines erudition with wit, offering historical context, explication of the text, and references connecting Mark's words to relevant sections of the Old and New Testaments. While not a formal commentary on Mark, this sermon series illuminates the Gospel, making its overall pattern clear and its message applicable to the present.

One does not often find a book that presents solid biblical teaching and scholarly explanation in clear, straightforward language leavened with colloquial anecdotes. Karl's *The Gospel According to St. Mark* is a pleasure to read and study and it will make a valuable addition to one's library of Christian literature.

Dr. Margaret Blom
Rector's Warden
Holy Trinity Anglican Church
Vancouver, BC, Canada

CONTENTS

Bible Reference	Page	Bible Reference	Page
1:1–15	1	10:1–16	129
1:16–39	7	10:17–31	137
1:40–2:17	13	10:32–45	143
2:18–3:6	19	10:46–52	149
3:7–35	25	11:1–11	155
4:1–20	31	11:12–19	161
4:21–34	37	11:20–33	167
4:35–41	43	12:1–12	173
5:1–20	49	12:13–27	179
5:21–43	55	12:28–37	185
6:1–29	61	12:38–13:2	191
6:30–44	67	13	197
6:45–56	73	14:1–11	203
7:1–23	79	14:12–26	209
7:24–37	85	14:27–52	215
8:1–21	91	14:53–72	219
8:22–30	97	15:1–20	225
8:31–9:1	103	15:21–47	231
9:2–13	111	16:1–8	237
9:14–32	117	16:9–20	243
9:33–50	123		

Mark 1:1–15, March 16th, 2014

We've spent the past six weeks looking at the opening chapters of Genesis. Today we start a sermon series looking at Mark's Gospel account. A ground-rule that I'm going to set myself — you can see how well I keep to it — is that I'm going to try not to say "Mark's Gospel": it isn't. It's, as most translations of Mk. 1:1 say, "The gospel of Jesus Christ" according to Mark; although the words "according to" can have a slightly apologetic ring to them. A friend of mine who was brought up on the Prayer Book thought that of the phrase in the Nicene Creed "according to the Scriptures". Perhaps the modern version, "in accordance with", is clearer on this point.

I heard the Sydney evangelist John Chapman say that in his experience Sydney Diocese clergy have a habit of starting a new ministry with a series on Mark. He speculated that this is what they're taught to do at Moore Theological College. There are good reasons to look at Mark early on though. Mark's, it is now generally accepted, is the earliest written of the Gospel accounts. The reason Matthew comes before it in our Bibles is because it was previously thought that Matthew was written first. And if you look hard enough, you'll find theologians who'll make a case for each of the four Gospel writers having been first. If you want to know the basis for the majority opinion, ask me afterwards. (It involves the mysterious character Q, not to be confused with James Bond movies!)

Also passé is the idea, prevalent in the nineteenth and the earlier twentieth century, that the Gospel accounts weren't written until the second century. The evidence now indicates that all four were first century compositions and Mark was written no later than AD 70, possibly as early as AD 50.

That still leaves the question, why did Mark wait twenty or so years before putting reed-pen to papyrus? An answer is that the earliest Christians thought that Jesus was going to return in their lifetime. When it became apparent that this was in fact unlikely to be the case, they wrote down what they knew so that the oral tradition could be reliably passed on. In the case of Mark, he largely drew upon Peter's preaching.

Richard Burridge, Dean of King's College, London, has written a very readable book, *Four Gospels, One Jesus?: A Symbolic Reading*. In it, he draws upon the four images traditionally associated with the four gospel writers or evangelists. Can anyone volunteer what those images are and, more trickily, which one goes with whom? It's actually a bit of a trick-question regarding which with whom. Before 398, Sts. Irenaeus and Augustine had a go, then Jerome came up with something different and that's what we have today.

Richard Burridge does a good job of expounding Mark's lion-like qualities. I have a friend who is wont to tell me, "Your problem is ... " At this point I usually interrupt and say, "You mean, one of my problems is ... " "Yes," says my friend, "One of your problems is that whereas I'm an Eeyore, I never expect anything to work and therefore I'm never disappointed, you're a Tigger. You bounce around all over the place with all your ideas and plans, and then you're disappointed when others don't fall into line and share your enthusiasm!" I know lions are different from Tiggers, but Mark has that bouncy quality about him; we never quite know where he's going to land next, leaping all over the place: fast, furious, frenetic, fantastic.

Look at how he starts: "The beginning of the gospel of Jesus Christ, the Son of God." Mark leaps onto the stage with a proclamation. What does gospel mean? The answer usually given is 'good news'. But *evangelion*, gospel, is a stronger word: it's great news, life-changing news.

Baptism was something with which the Jews were familiar. It represented repentance, confessing sins. But John's baptism was limited. Sin could be confessed but there wasn't forgiveness or new life on offer: that required Jesus. "I [John] baptise you with water, but he [Jesus] will baptise you with the Holy Spirit", v. 8.

Why was Jesus baptised? Did he need to be? Not on his own account, for he was without sin. But his baptism heralded the beginning of his public ministry. And right here we get an indication of where that was to lead: his death on our behalf on the cross. Jesus, through his baptism, fully identifies with our human state, just as he did through his temptation in the desert. It wasn't his sin that he was being baptised for, it was ours.

The question of baptism was raised at our Lent study group last Thursday. I want to share with you some of the things we talked about. We are told that Jesus was baptised by John in the River Jordan and that Jesus came up "out of the water." The only thing that we can be sure of from this is that water is involved in baptism, not how much nor that Jesus necessarily was totally immersed in it. There's evidence that while Jews baptised at this time may have stood in a river, the water would have been poured over them.

As for the nature of the water, I recommend that it be warm, especially where babies are concerned! We use ordinary tap water, just as John used river water. In Acts ch. 8, v. 36 we read, "As they travelled along the road, they came to some water and the eunuch said, 'Look, here is water. Why shouldn't I be baptised?' " And he was, in some water they found by the roadside. The Baptism service in the Book of Alternative Services provides for 'Thanksgiving over the Water' and that is what we do. We say, "sanctify this water" which means we're going to set it aside for a holy purpose, but it remains water nonetheless, just as the water in the Jordan did as it flowed on.

The prayer continues: "sanctify this water that your servants who are washed in it may be made one with Christ in his death and resurrection, to be cleansed and delivered from all sin." The water is an "outward and visible sign of [the] inward and spiritual grace" of accepting Jesus as our Lord and Saviour. In the case of an adult, baptism follows a public profession of faith; for infants it is done on the basis of the faith of the parents in the hope that in time the child will come to accept that faith as his own.

At Jesus' baptism, God speaks. A hallmark of conservative, traditional Christianity is that we believe God speaks into our situation. Have you ever had someone say to you that God has spoken to him, she has a message from the Lord? I have. It can be somewhat disconcerting. How can one argue with someone who apparently has a hotline with God?

There are instances in the Bible, such as here, when God speaks audibly: v. 11, "A voice came from heaven." But I think it's significant that whenever God speaks in this way in the New Testament, he always quotes from the Old Testament. It's as if he's saying, 'If you want to hear what I've got to say, read it, in the Bible.' There were indeed prophets in the Old Testament, who spoke on God's behalf. And we can see John the Baptist as the last in the line of those prophets. But now that we have the Bible in its completeness, the way we hear God speaking to us is through its pages. And through proclamation, the ministry of preaching. So my question regarding someone who claims to have a message from God is, 'What does the Bible say on the matter?' If the Bible is clear regarding a situation, then yes, we can be sure of hearing God speaking.

What are God's words on this occasion? I'm going to invite you to read them aloud with me. V. 11, "You are my Son, whom I love; with you I am well pleased."

God quotes first from Ps. 2, v. 7, "He said to me, 'You are my Son.' " And who is the one of whom God says this? Every Jew would have been able to answer this from Ps. 2, v. 2, "His Anointed One". Who is the Anointed one? The Messiah: that's what Anointed One means. And Messiah and Christ are the same word: one Hebrew, one Greek. God is saying, this is my Son, the Messiah, the Christ. What was the Messiah to do? Again, any Jew could tell you: he was to rule and put the world right; marking an end to injustice and the beginning of a reign of peace.

And God also quotes Is. 42, v. 1, regarding Jesus, "Here is my servant, whom I support. Here is my chosen one, with whom I am pleased" (GWT). God tells us not only who Jesus is: his Anointed One, the Messiah, the Christ, who is to put the world right. But he says how Jesus is to achieve this: as the suffering servant of whom Isaiah had prophesied. Is. 53, v. 5, "He was pierced for our transgressions, he was crushed for our iniquities; the punishment that brought us peace was upon him." Again, a vision of the cross, that was to be the outcome and culmination of Jesus' ministry. The cross was no accident: it's right there at the beginning of Jesus' ministry, at his baptism.

God says one more thing of Jesus, and it's deeply personal: "You are my Son, whom I love." This speaks to us of how much our redemption is to cost God in personal terms. And how much he loves us. How do you know how much someone loves you? By how much it costs him to do so.

Mark is a man with an urgent message for us. And so he quotes Jesus: v. 15, " 'The time has come,' he said. 'The kingdom of heaven is near. Repent and believe the good news.' " This gospel demands a response if it is to be good news. John had preached repentance and so does Jesus. But Jesus offers us more. Believe that I am the Messiah, the Christ, God's anointed, chosen one. And through belief in my death on your behalf as the suffering servant, your sins will be forgiven and you will be baptised with the Holy Spirit.

Amen.

Mark 1:16–39, October 15th, 2017

A word about the sermon series we're beginning today. It might be headed 'mind the gap.' We spent two years, from March 2014 to April last year, working our way through Mark's Gospel account, every chapter and verse (it was interspersed with series from the Old Testament and Epistles). I'm intending to gather all my sermons on Mark together in a book; it might even be available for Christmas, an excellent stocking-filler! But there were gaps when I didn't preach, because someone else did; and that's what this series will be filling in, hence, mind the gap.

Please turn to our passage, which you'll find on p. 968 of the church Bibles, Mk. ch. 1, beginning at v. 16.

"As Jesus walked by the Sea of Galilee." Regarding "Sea of Galilee" my NIV Study Bible says, "A beautiful *lake*...14 miles long and 6 miles wide." I think of it as too small to be a sea and too large to be a lake, hence it gets referred to as both.

Jesus is God, but he's also a man, every bit as human as you or I, except in regard to sin. He did the type of things we do: he went for a walk by the lake. Let's not forget either Jesus' divinity or his humanity.

"He saw Simon and his brother Andrew casting a net into the lake, for they were fishermen." So far, so ordinary: a pleasant walk by a lake and a scene of rural industry. Simon and Andrew were "casting a net into the lake, for they were fishermen" and that's what fishermen do, and, particularly in that day, might be expected to continue to do for the rest of their working life.

But then Mark, or rather Jesus, turns things upside down. V. 17: " 'Come, follow me,' Jesus said, 'and I will make you fishers of men.' " I wonder if you've become so used to those words, with their wordplay, that they lose their impact.

Admittedly, we know from Jn. 1 that this was not the first time Simon and Andrew had encountered Jesus; but nonetheless, people strolling by lakes don't usually go up to those going about their business and say, "Come, follow me" followed by, I've got another job for you to do, one, despite the wordplay, that's in fact quite different from what you've been used to. Which makes their response all the more startling. V. 18: "At once they left their nets and followed him." "At once", no hesitation, no turning back.

As if to emphasise the occurrence, it then happens again, this time with James and John. V. 20: "Without delay he called them, and they left their father Zebedee in the boat with the hired men and followed him."

What is going on here? Two things, I think. First, it speaks of Jesus' authority. It's not showy charisma; all Jesus does is call them, there are no fine words of persuasion. And it also speaks of an ability to recognise that authority and obey it, immediately: "At once ... Without delay."

In the words of the John Bell hymn:

> Will you come and follow me if I but call your name?
> Will you let my love be shown, will you let my name be known?
> Lord, your summons echoes true when you but call my name.
> Let me turn and follow you and never be the same.

Jesus calls people. Even unlikely people such as Simon, Andrew, James, John, you, me. Can you hear Jesus calling your name? How have you responded?

I was a member of the Christian Union (the Inter-Varsity group) when I was a student at Durham. Someone came up for his first term. He'd never heard the Gospel, knew little or nothing of Christianity. But when he heard about Jesus, through the CU, he responded immediately. Admittedly, there were a lot of gaps that needed to be filled in, as there are for all of us on an ongoing basis, and I'm not excluding myself from that. But he became a Christian, a follower of Jesus as Lord and Saviour, and he was glad to be so.

On my recent holiday, I bought a copy of *god is not Great* by the atheist Christopher Hitchens, from a book sale at a Massachusetts public library. It's the type of book that I'd never buy new, but for which I'm willing to shell out a dollar for a good cause.

At first, I'll admit to being a bit intimidated by Hitchens' apparent erudition; he spins a good yarn: talk about showy words of persuasion. I'm now halfway through the book and am less impressed. It appears that despite Hitchens' sophistication, or perhaps because of it, he's either never encountered the form of biblical Christianity I believe, as championed by Martin Luther at the Reformation, or hasn't understood it, or else is choosing to ignore it.

Friends, being a Christian involves recognising Jesus' authority and the authority of the Bible that tells us about him. And it involves responding to Jesus with obedience. There are people who have yet to get to first base in their knowledge of Jesus, who he is, what he has done. In the words of the Ethiopian eunuch of Acts 8, "How can I ... unless someone explains it to me?" [Acts 8:31]. In Paul's words in Rom. 10, "how can they believe in the one of whom they have not heard? And how can they hear without a preacher?" [Rom. 10:14].

" 'Come, follow me,' Jesus said, 'and I will make you fishers of men.' " Are you a follower of Jesus? Have you accepted him as your personal Lord and Saviour? If you have, how are you faring in the 'fishing' business? Are you willing to share with others, for their sake, what Jesus means to you; what you have learnt from your reading of the Bible? If nothing else, it's a matter of being willing to say, "Would you like to come to church with me?" Fishing just involves asking the question. As the prophet Isaiah says, "How beautiful ... are the feet of those who bring good news" [Is. 52:7].

"You don't have to go to church to be a Christian" is a fancy way of saying "I follow Christ except for where He goes." Where did Christ go? V. 21: "when the Sabbath came, Jesus went into the synagogue." Jesus went to church and "people were amazed at his teaching, because he taught them as one who had authority" [v. 22]. Are you willing to let yourself be amazed, dazzled by Jesus: what he says, who he is, what he has done, for you; in the words of a book by Marcus Borg: meeting Jesus again for the first time.

Jesus was to get into trouble for healing on the Sabbath, but that was later, and with the Jewish religious leaders, after word had got around. At this stage, as probably even later with the ordinary folk, people were just amazed.

There's an irony that the evil spirit knows exactly who Jesus is, and fears him with justification for that reason; whereas others choose not to. Evil is responsible for everything that is wrong with the world, not least suffering and death. The evil spirit cries out, "Have you come to destroy us?" To which the answer is yes, that's exactly why Jesus has come. He has the authority required to cast out all the evil in the world. Currently that's still a work in progress, to be completed upon Jesus' return in glory.

Again there's another quick-fire demonstration of Jesus' authority, this time involving healing of someone who was at death's door. V. 30: "Simon's mother-in-law was in bed with a fever, and they told Jesus about her. So he went to her, took her hand and helped her up. The fever left her and she began to wait on them." Now that's what I call a healing!

My mother had a series of bouts of illness that took her to hospital during the last two years of her life. On one occasion, I visited her. Although she was delirious, she told me to have something to eat: "There's plenty of food in the fridge." I guess that's what mothers and mothers-in-law are like, throughout time the world over.

The people waited until after sunset because it was the Sabbath, before bringing "to Jesus all the sick and demon-possessed." "He would not let the demons speak because they knew who he was", v. 34. It's not that the demons knew he was Jesus of Nazareth, that was no secret, but that he was "the Holy One of God": the Messiah, the Christ, which are the same thing, one in Hebrew, one in Greek. The so-called Messianic Secret: Jesus didn't want word to get out too soon, because he had three years of ministry to do, before who he was would lead, inevitably, to his death.

V. 38: "Jesus replied, 'Let us go somewhere else, to the nearby villages, so I can preach there also. That is why I have come.' " A clergy colleague in this diocese said to me, "You have a teaching emphasis in your preaching." A friend, who listened to a recording of one of my sermons, and has a preference for Greek-derived terminology, said, "It's very didactic." It's been said twice, so it must be true.

In my naivety, for I do have that quality, a bishop once described it I think as attractive, or was it endearing, naivety, I was a bit surprised by the comment; as I was by my theological college's description of me as "Christocentric [Christ-centred] in his theology." Er, what's the alternative, I thought.

What did Jesus do in the synagogue? He taught. Why did Jesus say he had come? To preach. I make no apology for being a preacher/teacher. That, for me, as, I believe, for Jesus, lies at the heart of pastoral ministry.

These miraculous events, recorded for us by Mark, are just a temporal taster of what Jesus will one day do upon his return. All of the people healed that day would become sick again and die. They still lived in a world under the shadow of death. It was only through Jesus' death and resurrection that evil, sickness and death could be dealt with. And we look forward to the consummation of this at Jesus' Second Coming.

When Jesus returns, it will be a day of both joy and judgement. It is good that he tarries in doing so, to give us and others time to prepare; to call more people to repentance and faith in him. Jesus' return, for those who put their trust in him, will herald the start not of temporary healing, but of eternal joy.

Amen.

Mark 1:40–2:17, March 30th, 2014

I've been in ordained ministry for ten years; I was ordained deacon in Sydney on March 14th 2004. I would want to emphasise that I've been in ministry for longer than that. As a Lay Reader, that is lay preacher, since 1992 and before that as a pew-dweller. One of the things the Episcopal Church gets right is its emphasis on lay ministry. Who are the ministers of the Church? "The ministers of the Church are lay persons, bishops, priests, and deacons": so says the Episcopal Church's catechism.

But since being ordained, I've found myself being sucked more and more into the strange world of the Church, or perhaps it's just a cumulative effect that longstanding lay church members can also attest to. One of the things I've discerned is an emphasis on pastoral ministry's being desirable in a cleric. So and so has a "pastoral heart" or "we're looking for a minister with a pastoral heart."

All well and good, who can argue with that? But my concern is the implication of what pastoral is limited to or, to put it another way, what it is seen as not being. If I were being provocative, I might say that pastoring gets reduced to being nice to people. More generously, it seems to involve empathy, being alongside people, and perhaps a certain amount of practical assistance. And it's contrasted with head-stuff: preaching, teaching, doctrine etc.

One of the things you sometimes see Christians wearing is a bracelet with WWJD on it: "What would Jesus do?" I'm sufficiently unsure of the validity of this question that I've never been tempted to wear one of these bracelets myself. I guess my reluctance is derived from my perception of Jesus' uniqueness; who am I to put myself in his place? But perhaps WDJD would be OK: what did Jesus do?

For an answer to this, I want first to refer to a verse just before our passage from Mark's Gospel account; Mk. ch. 1, v. 38: Jesus said to Simon and his companions, "Let us go ... to the nearby villages, so that I can preach there also. That is why I have come."

A fairly significant statement: Jesus telling his disciples and, via Mark, us, why he had come. I discern two aspects: Jesus' ministry was peripatetic, he wanted to reach as many people as possible, so he moved from place to place; and that ministry consisted of, as he himself said, preaching: "That is why I have come."

With that in mind, let's turn our attention to the three incidents that form the passage we're addressing today. There are two healings; first, that of a man with leprosy. V. 40, "A man with leprosy came to Jesus and begged him on his knees, 'If you are willing, you can make me clean.' Filled with compassion, Jesus reached out his hand and touched the man. 'I am willing,' he said. 'Be clean!' Immediately the leprosy left him and he was cured."

How do we categorise this? It's got those elements we're told are part of pastoral encounters. Jesus meets the man 'where he's at', he meets his need and, perhaps above all, there's that word 'compassion': what could be more pastoral than that? And this seems to be confirmed if we look at how other versions of the Bible translate the word: pity and sympathy; Jesus felt sorry for him; deeply moved; deep concern; loving-pity.

But there's always a problem when we try to capture the meaning of a word from another language, in this case New Testament Greek. And some other Bible versions do so quite differently: incensed; anger; indignant. If you're willing to accept my proposition that these meanings need to be put alongside compassion, what happens to our perhaps somewhat cosy vision of a pastoral encounter? Are such sentiments to be found in nondirective counselling training? I don't think so!

If we were to reduce the incident to a purely human encounter, are we forced to think of Jesus as being incensed, angry and indignant with the man? Or is something else going on that we need to factor in? Why might Jesus be angry? Against what is his anger directed?

If you had cause to visit a funeral director, you'd probably be offered a file of what would be considered helpful wise words, nowadays increasingly from sources other than the Bible. I suspect that what Henry Scott Holland wrote would be found there: "Death is nothing at all. I have only slipped away to the next room." How polite can I be in saying what I think about this, given the context in which I'm speaking? I think if someone were to say such things to me in my bereavement, I'd be tempted to say, "No, I've checked, she's definitely not in the next room."

The man with leprosy was not dead, but his condition was that of one who was as good as: he was effectively one of the walking dead. Yes, Jesus was filled with compassion, but at the same time he was incensed, angry and indignant, at disease and death. As I've said before, death is not natural, it was not God's intention for us, but entered into our experience as a result of the Fall of man, dating back to Adam and Eve.

"I am willing," says Jesus. And he's not only willing, he's also able. Able at that moment, for that man, to do something about the effect of the Fall as it manifested itself on that individual. V. 42, "Immediately the leprosy left him and he was cured." The nature of the healing, an encounter with the divine, a profound restoration, is emphasised by its immediacy and Jesus' injunction, v. 44, "Go, show yourself to the priest and offer the sacrifices that Moses commanded."

Now the scene switches to Capernaum and it's a paralytic rather than a leper. Why was he brought, and with some determination at that! I think we may presume that the man's friends perceived his need in much the same way that the leper had perceived his: he was suffering from a physical affliction; could something be done about it? Jesus' response? V. 5, "Son, your sins are forgiven."

We're not told what the paralytic and his friends made of this. Perhaps they were disappointed, perhaps bemused: this wasn't really what they'd gone to so much trouble for. As for the Teachers of the Law, they were apoplectic. V. 7, "He's blaspheming! Who can forgive sins but God alone?"

Then comes the sought-for healing: v. 12, "He got up, took his mat and walked out in full view of them all." I have a slight inkling of what it might be like to be paralysed, having been under a general anaesthetic. I was wheeled back into the ward on a trolley, thanked the porters and went to get up in order to get into my bed. Then I found I couldn't, I had no control over my limbs. "Not so fast," said the porters as they lifted me up and placed me in the bed. But not only was a man who, we may presume, had been paralysed for some time, able to get up of his own accord, he even carried his mat!

Why did Jesus heal the man? Again, I'm sure that Jesus was "filled with compassion." But that's not the reason he gives. V. 9, "That you may know that the Son of Man has authority on earth to forgive sins ... get up." It's not just a matter of dealing with the presenting physical issue, why the man had been brought, but also the underlying spiritual need. And Jesus is able and willing to deal with this as only he, the Son of Man, can.

On to our third scene, Jesus having dinner at Levi's house. Again, the Teachers of the Law, Pharisees, are in on the act with their two pennies' worth. V. 16, "Why does he eat with tax collectors and 'sinners'?" they asked. To which Jesus gives his answer, v. 17, "It is not the healthy who need a doctor, but the sick. I have not come to call the righteous, but sinners."

There are hymnbooks that allocate hymns to certain sections. The problem with this is some feel it's not proper to sing a particular hymn other than at say Epiphanytide. A favourite hymn of mine is 'At even, ere the sun was set.' I suspect that it won't be familiar to you because even I find it difficult to justify singing it other than at an evening service and we don't have one, as yet! These are selected lines from it:

> At even, ere the sun was set,
> The sick, O Lord, around Thee lay;
> O, in what divers pains they met!
> O, with what joy they went away!
>
> Once more 'tis eventide, and we,
> Oppressed with various ills, draw near.
>
> And none, O Lord, have perfect rest,
> For none are wholly free from sin.
>
> Thy kind but searching glance can scan
> The very wounds that shame would hide.
>
> Thy touch has still its ancient power.
> No word from Thee can fruitless fall;
> Hear, in this solemn evening hour,
> And in Thy mercy heal us all.

The greatest tragedy is that of the Teachers of the Law, the Pharisees, those who fail to see their need of Jesus' healing touch and word. Others may know that they need something, but what? And they provide a ready market for self-help gurus and books.

I wonder what it's like to be a doctor in the age of the Internet. "I know what's wrong with me, I read it on the web. Give me x, please." Or how about, "This is the problem with our church, if only we did x or y, all would be well."

Jesus couldn't help the Teachers of the Law, the Pharisees. They didn't even get to first base: admitting they had a problem he could address. Others came to him or were brought to him and were surprised. They knew they had a problem. But like the skilful doctor he was, he diagnosed the real problem and met their real need.

In the parish where I was the curate, we had Lay Readers and Ivy, the Pastoral Assistant. Ivy explained to me that she had pastoral skills whereas the Lay Readers didn't; they had been trained only to preach and teach. I didn't dare ask how she regarded the clergy in this respect!

I worry though about those who think they can be pastoral without needing to know the Bible. It's one thing to write a sermon with time and books available. But if you're in a pastoral situation with only empathy available as means of diagnosis and treatment, are you in danger of selling the Church short, failing to discern a real need, and failing to meet it?

I'm unsure of 'What would Jesus do?' bracelets and as I've said, I've never felt called to wear one. Because we're not Jesus and we're not called to be. But along with knowing what Jesus has done, in his ministry which we learn in the Bible, and, derived from this, through experience of his ministry in our own life, we should be able to answer the question, "What can Jesus do?" for a particular person, for a particular situation.

Jesus said, "Let us go ... so I can preach ... That is why I have come." Preaching and teaching from the Bible is an essential part of pastoring. To be an effective pastor is to be first and foremost a Bible-based preacher-teacher. Who are the ministers of the Church? We all are. You don't need a label or title to be able to offer pastoral support, other than that of Christian, a follower of Jesus, one who was in need and has found that need, that deepest need, met in and by him. But the more we know of Jesus from the Bible and the more, through this, we allow him to minister to us in our need, the more effective we will be in helping others find the one who is willing and able to meet their real need.

Amen.

Mark 2:18–3:6, April 6th, 2014

Mk. ch. 2, v. 18, the beginning of our passage: "Now John's disciples and the Pharisees were fasting. Some people came and asked Jesus, 'How is it that John's disciples and the disciples of the Pharisees are fasting, but yours are not?' "

The Pharisees were Jews who, of course, sought to follow, to comply with, the Old Testament; that was their worldview. I've previously described John, and it's John the Baptist that we're referring to here, as being the last of the Old Testament prophets. The Old Testament, particularly the latter part, is imbued with the sense of looking forward to, waiting for, the coming of the Messiah, God's anointed one, whom we also know as the Christ; it's the same word, one Hebrew, the other Greek.

That's what, in theory at least, the Pharisees were doing. Their religious practices were in preparation for something that was to come. I wonder if you can relate to the concept that you're so looking forward to something and preparing so assiduously for it, when it actually arrives ... well, it's a bit of a disappointment. Perhaps you wear yourself out preparing, so you're too exhausted to enjoy the event itself.

I wonder this sometimes about wedding preparations. So much effort seems to go into them nowadays, in terms of reception arrangements, the key determinate of the date, venues, colour schemes, transport etc., etc., and over an extended period of preparation; is there a risk of losing sight of what the marriage is actually about? The very fact that the term wedding is used rather than marriage is telling. Oh for the good old days when the preparation was the three weeks that banns were read!

What if your particular rôle in a situation is so identified with preparation that then you're left feeling, 'What do I do now?' Or you get used to thinking of your rôle as that of saving the day, manning the fort in the face of imminent disaster, but then the problem is fixed. Do you rejoice that it is so, or feel redundant?

John preached a baptism of repentance, and fasting was part of that. But that was all he had to offer: baptism with water, not the Holy Spirit. He could convince you of your sins but by what means were they to be forgiven?

The Pharisees were very good at identifying wrongdoing. Their solution was a mixture of trying to avoid wrongdoing in the first place and adherence to the Old Testament's sacrificial and purification system for lapses. But life gets very complicated if you understand sin purely in terms of doing: having done something wrong, then doing something to try to put it right.

Martin Luther, who in 1517 was the initiator of the Reformation of the Church, had found this. He had become a monk, hoping through this to find peace with God. But instead he became more and more distraught. He bought into, literally, all the Church of the day had to offer in terms of dealing with sin. In 1511 he went on a pilgrimage to Rome, ascended the Scala Sancta on his knees and was presented with an indulgence, a piece of paper remitting sins, for having done so. But disillusionment set in.

I got into conversation with Sylvia, not one of our church members, on Friday. Sylvia told me she liked Jesus: he was a good man. But she didn't believe what the Church taught about him. After all the Bible was only written by men; and the fact that it was men seemed important to her. But there's a slight problem here because the source for the bits that Sylvia says she likes about Jesus is also the Bible.

The Pharisees didn't have the issue of whether they believed what the New Testament says about Jesus. It hadn't been written but rather was being lived out before them. There was Jesus in person. They did however, have the issue of whether they believed what the Old Testament said about him. Was he the Messiah?

C.S. Lewis, the 20th century Christian writer, said, using St. Anselm of Canterbury's formula, "A man who was merely a man and said the sort of things Jesus said would not be a great moral teacher. He would either be a lunatic — on the level with the man who says he is a poached egg — or else he would be the Devil of Hell. You must make your choice. Either this man was, and is, the Son of God, or else a madman or something worse."

In our passage, Jesus describes himself two ways: the bridegroom, v. 20, and the Son of Man, v. 28. And both times, the Pharisees would have known exactly what he was saying and they didn't like it. When they heard 'bridegroom' they would have thought of Isaiah's prophecy: "For your Maker is your husband — the Lord Almighty is his name — the Holy One of Israel is your Redeemer; he is called the God of all the earth", Is. 54, v. 5. And 'Son of Man' would send them to Daniel's vision: "there before me was one like a son of man, coming with the clouds of heaven. He approached the Ancient of Days and was led into his presence. He was given authority, glory and sovereign power; all peoples, nations and men of every language worshiped him. His dominion is an everlasting dominion that will not pass away, and his kingdom is one that will never be destroyed", Dan. 7, vv. 13 and 14.

Fasting was what John's disciples had taken upon themselves as a means of preparation for the coming of the Messiah, the bridegroom, the Son of Man. The Pharisees had made quite an art of it. The Old Testament actually only specified fasting once a year, on the Day of Atonement. But the Pharisees chose to do so twice a week.

Jesus was asked why his disciples weren't fasting. He turns the question on its head: "You're asking me why my disciples aren't fasting. Er, I want to know why the others are when I'm here!"

I'm going to suggest — and this is the Rector speaking, not Jesus! — that not only was it unnecessary and inappropriate for John's disciples and the Pharisees to be fasting when the event they were awaiting had arrived, the coming of the Messiah, the Christ, but that actually the fasting, meant as preparation, was getting in the way of their recognising Jesus for who he was. They'd got so used to fasting that it became what it was all about.

I am an evangelical Anglican and Holy Trinity Church is known as being evangelical. You'll also hear the term 'low church'; evangelicals are typically 'low church'. What does that mean? Well, certainly not 'smells and bells'. Part of being evangelical or low church is simplicity in the form of service. Ceremonial worship used to be viewed as somehow vaguely not very British; foreign, Romish practices. I don't think that a very sound reason for eschewing them. The greater danger is they become an end in themselves.

I've been somewhat taken aback by all the rubrics that have appeared in the Book of Alternative Services. All sorts of instructions or, more subtly, suggestions. At a particular service on a particular day, this or that is to be done. And Father McCausland's Order of Divine Service adds to that. I am reminded of what Cranmer wrote in the Prayer Book's Preface about the need for reform (you'll find it, somewhat illogically, at the back of the Canadian version): "The number and hardness of the rules ... was the cause ... that many times there was more to find out what should be read, than to read it when it was found out." Coventry Cathedral used to have the words "Profound silence" inserted at various points in its liturgy. I feel that were Jesus and his disciples to arrive at such a moment they would be frowned upon for disturbing the profundity!

Jesus talks of not sewing "a patch of unshrunk cloth on an old garment", v. 21, and not pouring "new wine into old wineskins", v. 22. Jesus is saying, I bring something radically new, that can't just be tacked on as if an optional extra. Jesus provides, as it were a totally new garment, a new wineskin. Practices belong to the world of old wineskins if they take our eyes off Jesus. Luther discovered that the answer to sin lies not in doing penance, but rather faith in Christ and being repentant.

The Prayer Book gives good guidance on this matter: "Christ's Gospel is not a Ceremonial Law, (as much of Moses' Law was,) but it is a Religion to serve God, not in bondage of the figure or shadow, but in the freedom of the Spirit; being content only with those Ceremonies which do serve to a decent Order and godly Discipline."

Verses 2:23 to 3:6 further illustrate the difference Jesus makes by reference to the Sabbath. The disciples had been accused by the Pharisees of "doing what is unlawful on the Sabbath." Actually, the disciples weren't breaking God's law, but rather they weren't following the Pharisees' rulebook regarding how the Sabbath should be kept. The purpose of the Sabbath was to enable rest and for God to be worshipped. But through their add-on rules, the Pharisees made the Sabbath a burden and an end in itself. Jesus said to them, v. 27, "The Sabbath was made for man, not man for the Sabbath. So the Son of Man is Lord even of the Sabbath."

And ch. 3 v. 1, Jesus goes into the synagogue. Why was he there? We may suppose that he was there for the reason people should have gone to the synagogue on the Sabbath: to hear God's Word and worship him. But others had another reason for being there; they were "looking for a reason to accuse Jesus", just as the Pharisees were who, apparently, had been lurking in the grainfields.

To Jesus' question, v. 4, "Which is lawful on the Sabbath: to do good or to do evil, to save life or to kill?", we're told that "they remained silent." But Jesus knew what lay in their hearts; v. 5, "He looked around at them in anger and [was] deeply distressed at their stubborn hearts." Anger and deep distress, the same mixture of emotions that we came upon in chapter 1 when Jesus was faced with the effect of leprosy on a man.

Jesus asked, "Which is lawful on the Sabbath: to do good or to do evil, to save life or to kill?" The Pharisees remained silent, but then answered through their actions: v. 6, "Then the Pharisees went out and began to plot with the Herodians how they might kill Jesus." An unholy alliance if ever there was one. The Pharisees, who opposed Roman rule, and the Herodians, who supported it, were locked in mutual contempt. But now they laid that aside in order to conspire together to kill Jesus.

The Pharisees fasted and followed their rulebook. They talked the talk of waiting for the Messiah. But when faced with him, he threatened that which they knew and had grown to rely upon. How sad that the things they thought would lead them to God actually kept them from him.

Amen.

Mark 3:7–35, April 14th, 2014

What is today called according to the Church's liturgical calendar? You're allowed to look in the Prayer Books in the pews for guidance, it's not cheating! The 1962 Canadian Prayer Book says: 'The Sunday next before Easter, commonly called Palm Sunday'. When Cranmer wrote the original Prayer Book, he wasn't going to have any of this Palm Sunday business, far too Roman! And as his Prayer Book was used in Canada before 1918, like as not if you'd been sitting in the pews of the Pine Street church back in 1917, the board would probably just say the 'Sunday next before Easter'.

Does anyone remember Mother Angelica? She's a Roman Catholic nun who used to have her own television show, sort of the equivalent of the televangelists. She would refer to things such as palm crosses as "holy reminders". The danger though is if they cease to be 'reminders' and become an end in themselves. Like the sermon illustration that sticks in your mind, but what was it meant to illustrate? A clergy friend tells of people who don't come to church but still want to have a 'lucky cross'.

The NIV Bible accurately heads the passage read on the Hemlock Street steps as "The Triumphal Entry". Branches, of unspecified nature, are mentioned, but you'd be hard pressed to say that's what the passage is all about. It's Jesus' 'triumphal entry' into Jerusalem. The 'added value' that palm crosses may give is to remind us that the same week, Holy Week, Jesus was to be crucified, as we'll commemorate on Good Friday.

Mt. 21, v. 9, "The crowds that went ahead of [Jesus] and those that followed shouted, 'Hosanna to the Son of David! Blessed is he who comes in the name of the Lord! Hosanna in the highest!' " Yet within that same week we read at ch. 27, v. 22, " 'What shall I do ... with Jesus who is called Christ?' Pilate asked. They all answered, 'Crucify him!' 'Why? What crime has he committed?' asked Pilate. But they shouted all the louder, 'Crucify him!' "

Something of a rollercoaster. Even if those who shouted 'crucify' weren't the same as those who had shouted 'hosanna', where were his supporters? They seem to have melted away. Perhaps they felt that Jesus had let them down. They'd wanted something from him and he hadn't delivered. Harold Wilson, British Prime Minister in the 1960s and 70s, said, "A week is a long time in politics." The same could be said of Holy Week.

But this theme, of people wanting something from Jesus which was not what he was about, is not confined to Holy Week. It goes on today; and it's to be found in other Gospel passages. And so I'd like us to turn our attention to our passage from Mk. ch. 3.

V. 7, "Jesus withdrew with his disciples to the lake and a large crowd followed. When they heard all he was doing, many people came to him." Rector Jesus, new kid on the block, was drawing the crowds. The churchwardens and Parish Council were delighted: success! Or was it?

When we read the Bible, we're in the hands of the translators. Now I'm going to ask you to trust me as I have a go at translating. "Because of the crowd [Jesus] told his disciples to have a small boat ready for him." Why so? What in v. 9 the NIV translates as "crowding", could be translated as "crushing" or "constricting". In v. 10, "pushing forward" could be "falling upon' or "attacking", and "touch" could be "grab". They're violent words. The crowd wanted something from Jesus: healing. And they would do anything to get it from him. But it wasn't what he was about; it wasn't his main purpose. And he saw the danger that the crowds would deflect him from that purpose. And so the boat was ready. And v. 12, "He gave [the evil spirits] strict orders not to tell who he was", echoing his words to the leper in ch. 1.

During the last couple of years of her life, my mother had several hospital admissions suffering from infections that meant that she was in a world of her own: delirium. Yet even in this, the maternal instinct was still there. I tried to feed her in hospital, but she wasn't happy because I wasn't eating: "There's plenty of food in the fridge, help yourself," she said to me.

I wonder what your relatives make of your involvement in the Church. My parents were glad of it but I wonder if they thought I was taking it a bit too seriously, and that was even before I got ordained! Jesus' family heard that because of his activities "he was not even able to eat" and, v. 21, "they went to take charge of him." Again, take charge is a mild translation; the Greek word is more violent: seize, take custody, restrain. In their eyes "He is out of his mind" and they wanted to 'section him', at least that's what it's called in the UK: you're to imagine them with a straightjacket.

And then there are the Teachers of the Law. They made the journey from Jerusalem in order to put a stop to what Jesus was up to, and in their eyes, v. 22, "He is possessed by Beelzebub."

Long before Holy Week, Jesus was faced with people who opposed him because their agenda was not his. The crowds that had followed him to Lake Galilee did so because they wanted something from him, healing, that was not his main focus. And things turned ugly as they sought to use him for their own ends: crushing, constricting, attacking. Jesus' family sought to seize and restrain him because in their eyes "He is out of his mind". And according to the Teachers of the Law, "He has an evil spirit".

If the crowds, his family, the Teachers of the Law got Jesus wrong, what was it that he was about? What was his agenda? Let me take us back to vv. 13 and 14, "Jesus went up on a mountainside and called to him those he wanted, and they came to him. He appointed twelve, designating them apostles, that they might be with him and that he might send them out to preach."

When you hear about going up a mountainside your ears should prick up: something's about to happen. After Moses had met with God on Mount Sinai, he "set up twelve stone pillars representing the twelve tribes of Israel", Ex. 24:4. That was the old Israel, whose leaders, as we read at the end of last week's passage, were plotting how they might kill Jesus. Now Jesus founds a new Israel, based on the twelve apostles he appoints.

Anyone submitting for ordination is more than likely to receive training in contextual ministry. We are to be sensitive and responsive to the context in which we seek to minister. And I've received such advice since moving here, for example from Michael Ingham just before the new bishop's consecration service. All well and good.

The problem comes if context takes over and we become just reflective of it. What then do we have to offer? I was told of a conversation regarding the choice of my successor as Vicar where I've come from: "We want someone who'll give us what we want." My successor's appointment was announced today and from what I know of her, she's someone whose priority is what God wants.

Jesus' take on contextual ministry might have caused him problems with the ordination process. He wasn't willing to submit to the consumerist approach of the crowds, his family and the Teachers of the Law: he didn't give them what they wanted.

In the Creed we state that "We believe in one holy catholic and apostolic Church." To say we believe in it means 'we're part of it'. The Church is apostolic when it adheres to the apostles' teaching, that which Jesus appointed the Twelve to preach. That was Jesus' agenda, for them and for us. And we should not allow ourselves to be deflected from it. We who are Christian, part of the apostolic Church, are part of the new Israel, one based not on being Jewish but rather on adherence to Jesus' teaching, Jesus' agenda.

I want to end with two notes of personal comfort. Jesus' family had been among those who opposed him. Mark is being honest and open by telling us this, because of course Jesus' family came to believe in him. His brother, James, became an important leader in the Jerusalem church: imagine what he might have to say if preaching on these verses from Mark's gospel account!

Paul writes to the church at Corinth, "The wicked will not inherit the kingdom of God ... And that is what some of you were. But you were washed, you were sanctified, you were justified in the name of the Lord Jesus Christ and by the Spirit of our God" I Cor. 6, vv. 9 and 11.

Think of the conversion of Paul himself. People can change, or rather, God can change people. And some of the fiercest opponents of Jesus can become his most stalwart followers.

I remember some wise words from a speaker at the Christian Union when I was a student at Durham University in the 1980s. Knowing what earnest students can be like, he told us, "If you're worried about having blasphemed against the Holy Spirit, you haven't done it!"

The Teachers of the Law said Jesus was possessed of Beelzebub, that is blasphemy against the Holy Spirit. To be Christian, a follower of Jesus, means, at its most basic level, saying 'No, you've got it wrong, upside down. Jesus because of who he is, God's son, is the one who casts out and does away with evil.'

I invite you, as followers of Jesus, to join me in affirming that and in adhering to and sharing the teaching of the apostles appointed by Jesus, his agenda.

Amen.

Mark 4:1–20, October 22nd, 2017

I suspect that today's passage is one of the better known in the Bible; better known in the sense of being something people have heard before, which doesn't necessarily mean better understood.

Back in the Dark Ages when I was at primary school, and there wasn't anything fancy about the school, just a run of the mill state school in Birmingham; but back then the 1944 Education Act was adhered to, and each day started with an assembly "of a broadly Christian nature." Broadly Christian meant it wasn't a time for proselytising by a particular denomination, although most of the children would have been nominally Church of England. But we were introduced to the Bible, and I can still remember the deputy head talking about the parable of the sower.

How grateful I am for that grounding, both at primary school and subsequently at secondary school. If children aren't hearing the Bible at school, and I suspect they aren't, where are they hearing it?

The deputy head referred to the passage as the parable of the sower. Indeed, that is the heading the NIV Bible gives to the passage, although remember that those headings, although generally helpful, are not part of the biblical text: that's why they're in italics. The image of the sower has been adopted by the Bible Society, and in Australia its magazine is called *The Sower*.

Last Sunday, when we looked at chapter 1, we had Jesus calling us to be fishermen. Now he takes the metaphor inland, for which, as someone from the heart of the English Midlands, I'm grateful, and we are to become farmers sowing.

But for this to make any sense, we need to have something to sow. The Bible Society recognises this because its logo equips the sower with a container strapped around his neck, from which he is dispensing seed; he's not an idle sower, but one actively engaged in sowing seed.

Where I was previously, we had a Church of England primary school, Archbishop Cranmer School no less. Someone from the Diocese came to lead a Godly Play session, which I heard about from the head teacher. The reason I heard about it, as the Vicar and a school governor, was that the head teacher was bemused. She'd asked the Godly Play person, "Aren't you going to explain what the parable means?" only to be told, "No, it's better that the children find their own meaning in it."

Needless to say, I was equally bemused by this. It seems a strange way of teaching, and I wonder how it transfers to other subjects: 'two plus two equals ... well children, it's up to you to come up with your own answers, all of which will be equally valid of course'. Perhaps that's the Ontario curriculum!

It's particularly baffling as this is an example of a parable that Jesus explains; he tells us what the seed represents, so there can be no doubt.

Please turn to the passage if you haven't already, you'll find it on p. 971 in the church Bibles, Mk. ch. 4.

V. 14: Jesus says, "The farmer sows the word." To not tell the children that the seed represents the word is a case of taking a text out of context. Presumably, Godly Play dealt only with vv. 3–8. But if you divorce these from vv. 9–20, you're being true neither to the Bible, nor to Jesus, and after all, he's the one speaking, it's his parable. Remember, a text taken out of context can be just a pretext.

The Canadian Bible Society, as well as having the image of a sower actively sowing seed, also has a magazine called *Word at Work*. This is helpful. What does the sower sow? The word. If we are to be any use as sowers, we must get to know our Bibles. That is what we are to be sowing: the word about Jesus, contained in the Bible.

I can suggest two helpful resources. The *NIV Study Bible*: everyone should have one; I find it indispensable, particularly when asked tricky questions! And Scripture Union's *Encounter with God* Bible reading notes, which we make freely available: ask for your copy.

So, the parable can be referred to as the parable of the sower; but equally it could be known as the parable of the seed, that which the sower sows, the word, God's Word, of the kingdom that Jesus came to bring.

Now, I'm going to suggest a third name for the parable, and remember, the Bible doesn't actually give it a name, so this is a case when all of them might be considered valid. Jesus depicts four scenarios of what might befall the seed sown. In each scenario, it's the same sower or farmer, and the same seed: there's no criticism of either the farmer or the seed. So what makes the difference? It's the ground on which the seed falls, and so I suggest it could be termed the parable of the soils.

Notice the emphasis on hearing. V. 3: Jesus begins, "Listen!" V. 9: "Then Jesus said, 'He who has ears to hear, let him hear.' " V. 12: "ever hearing but never understanding." And the word "hear" occurs four more times in the course of Jesus' explanation in vv. 15–20.

V. 15: Jesus says, "Some people are like seed along the path, where the word is sown. As soon as they hear it, Satan comes and takes away the word that was sown in them." We might like to think of birds such as a dove, representing peace or the Holy Spirit, or an eagle, the symbol of John the Evangelist. Here, I'm afraid they're seen in a rather more Hitchcockian light, as representing Satan.

The people who receive the seed, the word, in this way, are those of whom it could be said, in one ear and out the other. They don't really hear, perhaps because they don't really listen, or perhaps because it all becomes just an intellectual game, idle amusement.

Then there's the seed that falls on rocky places with little soil and no chance for roots. V. 16: Jesus says, "Others, like seed sown on rocky places, hear the word and at once receive it with joy. But since they have no root, they last only a short time. When trouble or persecution comes because of the word, they quickly fall away."

This, I'm afraid, speaks of too much of today's Church: shallowness, perhaps accompanied by a certain amount of hype or emotionalism. A Church that may be a mile wide, but is only an inch deep. A major theme of my ministry is trying to ensure this isn't the case in the places of which I have charge. The motto of St. Anselm, Archbishop of Canterbury at the turn of the twelfth century, is "faith seeking understanding." We need be grownup as Christians, something with which St. Paul would certainly agree.

One of my messages is that tough times will come, bad things happen to Christians as well. In fact, the evidence is that persecution of Christians is on the rise: today's western society is not as tolerant as it likes to think it is, certainly not when it comes to Christian belief and mores.

V. 18: Jesus says, "Still others, like seed sown among thorns, hear the word; but the worries of this life, the deceitfulness of wealth and the desires for other things come in and choke the word, making it unfruitful." The Bible repeatedly tells us not to worry or be afraid. Why does it do so? Because it knows of our propensity to worry, admittedly more so in the case of some than others.

The only way of getting rid of a Rector in the Church of England, certainly one who has the freehold, is on a charge of "conduct unbecoming." This has been reduced basically to matters concerning sex or money. But, let's face it, these are major temptations, and areas in which many go astray: "the deceitfulness of wealth and the desires for other things."

I find myself thinking, from time to time, should I have remained at the *Express & Star* newspaper back in 1989, with a solid career ahead of me. What of my pension, will I be in penury? Where will I live? What foolish thoughts, compared with the riches of knowing that one is serving Christ in the way he calls us to do.

Jesus says, Mt. 6:24, "No one can serve two masters. Either you will hate the one and love the other, or you will be devoted to the one and despise the other. You cannot serve both God and money. Therefore I tell you, do not worry about your life, what you will eat or drink; or about your body, what you will wear. Is not life more than food, and the body more than clothes?"

Now we come to the "good soil", those who, v. 20: "hear the word, accept it, and produce a crop." Alleluia, grain at last! Those who not only "hear the word" but "accept it", embrace it, and go on to be fruitful Christians. This speaks of our justification, accepting Jesus as Lord and Saviour, and our sanctification, growing in holiness through the indwelling of the Holy Spirit.

But note that, even here, the crop varies: "thirty, sixty, or even a hundred times what was sown." You may be a Christian, having given your life to Christ; your salvation is secure through Christ's sacrifice on your behalf, but are you letting the Holy Spirit do his ongoing work in your life? It is regarding that that we, even as Christians, will be judged.

It's not apparent in our English translation, but in the Greek original, there's a difference between the tense of the verb "hear" in v. 20, referring to the good soil, and the form it appears in with regard to the other three 'soils'. To be technical, the earlier forms are punctiliar or aorist: the hearing action is one-off. For those who are Christian however, the hearing of the word needs to be ongoing, linear; we need to hear and keep on hearing.

The parable can be seen as a parable of a sower. We are called to be sowers, just as we are called to be fishermen: the Department of Agriculture and Agri-Food Canada should be pleased! Perhaps Godly Play takes too literally, and again out of context, Jesus' words in v. 11 about "The secret of the kingdom of God". To quote Doris Day: "Once I had a secret love ... Now I shout it from the highest hills ... And my secret love's no secret anymore."

At the beginning of ch. 4 we read, "The crowd that gathered around [Jesus] was so large that he got into a boat and sat in it out on the lake, while all the people were along the shore at the water's edge." Jesus was willing to teach any who came across his path, regardless of whether they were willing to hear his word and accept it.

I become somewhat exasperated with an attitude that says there are some people who are likely targets for coming to church, and others who aren't worth bothering with. That is not the message of the sower.

The sower/farmer spreads the word/seed liberally. We don't know who are going to respond and who not. Sometimes it's the unlikeliest people who do so. Sometimes there's no immediate response but it comes later, sometimes much later. Sometimes, it's the people who give us the most grief who are the ones who are actually searching. If God puts someone across our path, it's for a reason. Be willing to strike up a conversation and see where it goes.

Let's assume that the conversation goes somewhere. Then make sure you have something to say. The parable of the word speaks of our knowing enough of the Bible to convey who Jesus is for you, and what he has done for you and can do for someone else.

Finally, the parable of the soils. Don't have unrealistic expectations. Three quarters of the seed appears to have fallen on unproductive ground. But equally, hold onto the promise that some of the seed sown will produce a crop, thirty, sixty even a hundredfold. If you never sow, you'll never know.

Amen.

Mark 4:21–34, June 22nd, 2014

We were fortunate to have Roger Simpson with us last week. And I'm pleased that he's agreed to continue to work with us at Holy Trinity. One of the questions that he addressed was, "Why should I evangelise?" I also want to look at that question today. Please turn in your Bibles to p. 972, Mk. ch. 4 v. 21, "[Jesus] said to them, 'Do you bring in a lamp to put it under a bowl or a bed? Instead, don't you put it on its stand?' " A friend of mine said to me, "Karl, you're always trying to convert me to something!" I guess I have that trait in me. If I discover something good, I want to share it.

You may not have my apparent zeal for sharing. But nonetheless, I bet you've done so. Think about something you discovered that was really good or useful or enjoyable. Didn't you want to tell someone about it? The present you gave because you'd found, whatever it was, to be helpful and you thought the person you were giving it to would find it so as well. Travellers meeting in a hostel share their experiences; tips on where to go, what to see. I spent a week in a hotel on a management course. About the only useful thing that came out of that as far as I was concerned was the barman recommending that I try Canadian Club!

Why do we do this, sharing our thoughts and experiences with others? Because we care for the other person.

Penn Jillette is an American comedian and illusionist and remains an avowed atheist. But he has gone on record as saying this:

I don't respect people who don't proselytise ... If you believe that there's a heaven and a hell ... and you think it's not really worth telling [people about] this ... how much do you have to hate somebody not to proselytise? How much do you have to hate somebody to believe that everlasting life is possible and not tell them that?

You can see a video of Penn Jillette talking more about this on the YouTube website (his train of thought was started after he was given the gift of a New Testament and Psalms).

I know of parents who say, "We're not going to influence our children regarding religion. We're going to leave it to them to make up their own minds." Yet all parents are constantly exerting influence on their children in the areas they think matter. In a way, I can respect more readily the parent who says, "I'm an atheist and I'm going to share this belief (and yes, it is a belief) with my child"; I can respect that more readily than the parent who admits there might be something in religion, but does nothing to help his child in this area. Of course, I'm delighted that Bradley and Claudine are having Brad baptised today as his first step in the Christian faith.

"[Jesus] said to them, 'Do you bring in a lamp to put it under a bowl or a bed? Instead, don't you put it on its stand?' " The gift God has entrusted to us is meant to be shared with others. Our knowledge of Jesus is light meant to shine into darkness. God entrusts the light of that knowledge to us. Jesus says to us, What are you doing with it? Are you keeping it to yourselves? Hiding it away as if under a bowl or bed? Or are you displaying what you know of me, so that others may benefit as well? That is my answer to the question, "Why should I evangelise?"

V. 24, "'Consider carefully what you hear,' [Jesus] continued. 'With the measure you use, it will be measured to you — and even more.' " I remember singing as a child:

> Love is like a magic penny,
> Hold it tight and you won't have any.
> Lend it, spend it, and you'll have so many
> They'll roll all over the floor.

Good advice for a new Christian is 'tell someone about your new faith.' In fact, tell at least three people. And I believe that this verse, "With the measure you use, it will be measured to you — and even more", says that in doing so, God will bless us. I sometimes hear people say, "I wish I had more faith". The way to increase your faith is to share it. And the more you do so, the easier it becomes.

I quoted the next section of our passage, vv. 26–29, in my Easter letter:

"[Jesus] also said, 'This is what the kingdom of God is like. A farmer scatters seed on the ground. Night and day, whether he sleeps or gets up, the seed sprouts and grows, though he does not know how. All by itself the soil produces grain — first the stalk, then the head, then the full kernel in the head. As soon as the grain is ripe, he puts the sickle to it, because the harvest has come.'"

Jesus points to growth as the work of two partners:

- the farmer gets the environmental factors right to maximise the potential for new life and growth by consistently removing the obstacles to healthy growth,

- but God alone brings that life and growth (which appears to happen as if "all by itself" to the farmer).

Our rôle is similar to that of the farmer. We cannot give life or produce growth. Only God can do that. But we can maximise the potential for growth. This is done by a continual process of identifying the barriers which impede growth within the life of the Church and removing them. In this way the potential for 'all by itself' growth is constantly maximised.

We will be engaging with a programme called Natural Church Development which is based on this principle. It emphasises that quality (health) should precede quantity in Church growth thinking. Becoming a 'healthier' Church prepares the ground for God to bring new life and growth. I hope that applying this to Holy Trinity will help us identify and address what we most need to work on as we move forward.

Jesus talked about seed at the beginning of the chapter in the Parable of the Sower. And he told the disciples what the seed represented in the parable: "the word", v. 14. He now returns to the seed analogy in v. 31 when teaching about the kingdom of God. And he says what sort of seed he has in mind: "It is like a mustard seed, which is the smallest seed you plant in the ground." In other words, it's quite likely to be dismissed as insignificant, unlikely to amount to much. "Yet," v. 32, "when planted, it grows and becomes the largest of all plants, with such big branches that the birds of the air can perch in its shade."

I told you in an earlier sermon how as a nineteen-year-old I was rather taken in by the Tower of Babel. Move forward ten years and I was a salesman in London: smart suit and leather briefcase. It was the late 1980s and all seemed to be success. I remember looking around at the glitz and again being well and truly taken in by it: "I see the sights that dazzle, the tempting sounds I hear." I thought, 'It doesn't get better than this.' I even bought shares in a bank: don't come to me for investment advice! For after the boom, came the bust. More significantly, I had found myself wanting to be involved with churches that were big and 'successful': lots of people, the best music, etc.

There were reminders of this at an event I attended elsewhere yesterday morning. We were asked to consider our 'creativity' in worship. The subsequent discussion led me to ask, "Who is to 'benefit' from this worship?" "The worshippers", was the response. And there was talk about "embarrassment" if the worship was not "up to scratch". "Who is embarrassed?" I asked. "We are," came the reply. Friends, to whom is our worship offered, who is the recipient? God. What does he look for? Success? Glitz? He looks into the heart. I Sam. 16, v. 7: "The Lord said to Samuel (when anointing the next king of Israel), 'Do not look on his appearance or on the height of his stature, because I have rejected him; for the Lord does not see as mortals see; they look on the outward appearance, but the Lord looks on the heart.'"

There are all sorts of things that look beguiling in the world's eyes; that are symbols of 'success'. God isn't interested in these. There are all manner of techniques and quick fixes that churches may be tempted to adopt. What does God provide? His word about Jesus contained in the Bible. It may seem insignificant, inadequate in the world's eyes, as insignificant as a mustard seed.

Yet it is from that, and only that, that God's kingdom is to be grown.

This is such an important principle and we find it repeated again and again. Who was Jesus? A wandering preacher, born in obscurity, who died an ignominious death. Whom did he choose as his disciples? Hardly the people the world would have chosen. As Paul writes, "The foolishness of God is wiser than man's wisdom, and the weakness of God is stronger than man's strength", I Cor. 1, v. 25.

I began by addressing the question "Why should I evangelise?" I end by addressing "Why should you evangelise?" To whom did Jesus address these three parables? Who was the 'them'? V. 1, "The crowd that gathered around [Jesus] was so large that he got into a boat and sat on it out on the lake, while all the people were along the shore at the water's edge." A crowd so inclusive that it includes you and me.

I recall preaching in one of my former parishes. Bernard was sitting there with a beatific smile upon his face. You know how I sometimes throw out questions when preaching. Bernard seemed so attentive that I decided to address one of my questions to him. No response. Then he realised he was the centre of my attention. "Wait a minute," he said, "I'll turn my hearing aid back on"!

Jesus says, v. 23, "If anyone has ears to hear, let him hear." I think the reason Jesus taught using parables was to seek to engage people's attention. I hope that I have engaged yours. To hear again, I refer you to our Facebook page!

Amen.

Mark 4:35–41, November 5th, 2017

Please turn to p. 972 in the church Bibles, where you'll find our passage, Mk. ch. 4, beginning at v. 35.

"That day when evening came, [Jesus] said to his disciples, 'Let us go over to the other side.'" I'm afraid this verse brings to mind the rather silly thing that I am apt to say from time to time. The last occasion I can recall was when about to enter security at Visby Airport, when I said to Martin, my travelling companion, "I'll see you on the other side." The joke being that "the other side" has other, perhaps more profound, implications.

Here, however, this is not the case. Indeed, the verse expresses the commonplace, and acts as a reminder that alongside Jesus' divinity, we must hold his humanity. As well as being fully God, he was as fully man as you or I. We're given details as to the time of day: "That day when evening came." "The other side" relates merely to the Lake or Sea of Galilee, Jesus' usual stomping-ground.

Why did Jesus wish to cross to "the other side"? The reason is intimated in the next verse: "Leaving the crowd behind." Jesus wished to be alone, or at least away from the 'madding crowd.' Jesus didn't have an inexhaustible supply of energy, as indeed none of us have.

V. 37: "A furious squall came up, and the waves broke over the boat, so that it was nearly swamped." The ferocity of the storm is indicated by the fact that Jesus' disciples, among whom were experienced fishermen, thought it likely that they would drown. Yet, "Jesus was in the stern, sleeping on a cushion." I take this as a sign of Jesus' state of exhaustion, to sleep through such a storm.

Jesus could be exhausted, as can we all. We do well to follow Jesus' example in such instances: we need to rest, we need our sleep; God dictates that it be so. Let none of us think of ourselves as superhuman.

I grew up with the advertising slogan, "A Mars a day helps you work, rest and play." I understand that originally it was to be only "work and play", perhaps reflective of "All work and no play makes Jack a dull boy." I'm glad that "rest" was added. Incidentally, it was a cause of disappointment when I realised, only in my thirties, that Mars bars were not, as I had hitherto thought, a British product. The power of advertising!

Having been woken by his disciples, v. 39, "[Jesus] got up, rebuked the wind and said to the waves, 'Quiet! Be still!' Then the wind died down and it was completely calm." Jesus was human, yet he was also divine; he was God in human form. Here he exerts his divine power and authority: 'be quiet and stay that way', "Then the wind died down and it was completely calm."

I have no reason to believe that this incident did not occur. Indeed there is no reason to do so, other that blind unbelief which, as William Cowper says in his hymn, "is sure to err and scan His work in vain."

> God moves in a mysterious way
> His wonders to perform;
> He plants His footsteps in the sea
> And rides upon the storm.

If God in Jesus can calm a storm in this way, which he of course can — it's in his nature as God to be above and beyond nature — then he can do anything. The Incarnation, the Resurrection: nothing is impossible to God.

The miraculous nature of Jesus' intervention is shown not so much in the wind's dying down, for that could be counted as mere coincidence, but in the fact that it was then "completely calm." Anyone who has experienced a storm at sea will know that it can take days for the waves to calm, even after the wind has abated.

V. 41: "[The disciples] were terrified and asked each other, 'Who is this? Even the wind and the waves obey him!'"

I, as we probably all do, have favourite hymns, although I like to think that I'm open to supplementing this. One of my favourites is 'King of the Universe', in part because it's sung to the tune of the Imperial Russian Anthem, which I like to think of being played when my grandfather was decorated by the last Tsar, which he was.

'King of the Universe' is a modified version of Henry Chorley's 1842 hymn 'God the All-terrible', words which somehow we feel inhibited from singing in this day and age. Perhaps they remind us too much of someone such as Ivan the Terrible, although Ivan Grozny is in fact better translated as Ivan the Formidable.

Is there more of a place for acknowledging the awesomeness of God, in its true sense, than we usually allow? "[The disciples] were terrified." I think in their place I would be at least awestruck. Indeed, knowing my nature, I think I'd be scared stiff. Remember, the disciples hadn't yet comprehended who Jesus was. The turning-point does not come until chapter 8, midway through Mark's gospel account.

But the disciples ask the right question: "Who is this? Even the wind and the waves obey him!" It's a question we need to ask and keep asking until we reach the right conclusion: Jesus is God, for only God can do what he does. The psalmist tells us that it is God alone who rules the rolling of the sea. Clearly, this event is pointing to Jesus as God come to earth.

So there we are, that's that. A passage dealt with in ten minutes. I must be a true Anglican! Except, did you notice, I skipped a verse? Come with me back to v. 40. Jesus has rebuked the wind, but it strikes me that he then goes on to rebuke the disciples: "Why are you so afraid? Do you still have no faith?" Ouch.

Whereas the disciples' terror in v. 41 relates to Jesus' being able to control wind and waves, I don't think this is what Jesus is referring to in v. 40. I think his comment goes back to what the disciples said to him when they woke him in v. 38: "Teacher, don't you care if we drown?"

What am I getting at? It can be easy to believe and trust in God when things are going well. When our prayers are answered in the way we want; when troubles don't beset us. Then, to quote Robert Browning, "God's in His heaven / All's right with the world!"

But what of when that's not the case? My friends, storm clouds will come, even to the best of us. And it's then that you hear people saying, "I lost my faith because ... " 'Never mind that terrible things happen to other people, I know that, I didn't expect them to happen to me.'

Jesus expects the disciples, and us, to trust him as calmly and certainly when he does nothing to help, as when he acts in power. That is the true test of discipleship.

It is easy to trust a God who works by miracles. Easy to put your faith in Christ when God wonderfully intervenes when we pray in Christ's name. The problem comes when heaven is silent. When the storm clouds come and threaten by wind and rain. Yet Jesus is seemingly asleep in heaven. Then, and only then, do we know whether we trust him or not. Jesus wants to be trusted when he is asleep and not just when he does his mighty miracles.

I was at an excellent conference last week, along with Ian and Priscilla. One of the speakers spoke against the allegorical interpretation of Scripture. To which my response was, I'm not so sure. Allegorical interpretation was overdone in the medieval period, to the exclusion of a straight reading of the text. But, to my mind, that doesn't negate it altogether; let's not throw out the baby with the bathwater.

This Sunday in particular we are called to pray for the persecuted Church. The early Church was persecuted and they came to see the boat the disciples were in as representing the Church, battered by the storms of persecution. While Christ is with his people, with his supernatural power, they will survive. The fact that Christ is with his Church means that we will be preserved from extinction. The Church will never perish, and it never has.

We see trials mount up, the testing come, the storm roll over the sky, the boat under tremendous pressure. We're almost up to the limit of what we can stand. The Church cries out to God, and the Lord appears to do nothing. We find ourselves saying to God, "Don't you care?"

The omnipotent Lord is always with his people. Of that, there is no doubt. But this omnipotence of his will often be hidden. After his Ascension, Jesus is not with us physically, doing these kinds of miracles. There will be times when we wonder whether Jesus is really concerned for us. Can he see us in our difficulties? We cry out to Jesus and many times these prayers are apparently not answered. It's precisely when the miracles do not occur, that Christ calls upon us to believe and trust him still.

Amen.

Mark 5:1–20, July 6th, 2014

I met Alfred for the first time yesterday. "Do you like the Beatles?" he asked me. And he asked in a way that indicated that he'd discerned that my answer was going to be 'yes'. Slightly disconcerted, I admitted that yes I did, but then felt the need to add some balance: "I also like Joni Mitchell and Simon and Garfunkel." All of this labels me as a child of the 1960s, musically at least: perhaps it's what comes of growing up with a sister who's thirteen years older. It was Simon and Garfunkel who introduced me to Frank Lloyd Wright. "So Long, Frank Lloyd Wright," they sang. "Architects may come and Architects may go and Never change your point of view. When I run dry, I stop awhile and think of you."

I wasn't here last week. For my previous break, I'd gone to Los Angeles. "Why are you going to a city?" John asked me. "You live in a city." Undaunted, my recent holiday was to Chicago: I guess I like cities! And while there, I took the opportunity to find out more about Frank Lloyd Wright, the character I'd heard about in a song and whose initial career as an architect had been in Chicago.

Frank Lloyd Wright was a Unitarian and one of his early commissions was to build a Unitarian Church, Unity Temple. It's a building that has beauty. A seminal building, just as F.L.W. was a seminal architect. I enjoyed being shown round it. But I also found it disturbing. The building was wrong in its presuppositions, just as, in my opinion, Unitarianism is wrong.

I'd been shown round by a church member. I waited until the tour was over before asking her, "What do you believe about Jesus?" "He's just a man." "And what about the Holy Spirit?" This got a shrug of the shoulders, then, somewhat defensively, "There's nothing in the Bible about the Trinity." I backed off at that point, after all, I was on holiday!

I've never been to a Unitarian service and so never heard one of their sermons. But as I looked at today's passage from Mk. ch. 5,

I found myself wondering what a Unitarian would make of it. Because my reading of it is a basis for my assertion that much as Unity Temple is interesting and even beautiful, it's flawed in the way that its underlying Unitarian philosophy is flawed.

As well as being architecturally interesting, Chicago is also associated for me with the effect of bad weather. My arrival in Vancouver from Boston in January was held up for two days because of snow in Chicago. On my recent visit, I arrived to a thunderstorm and my departure was delayed by five and a half hours because of another. Last week you heard about another storm, at the end of Mk. ch. 4, which Jesus quelled by his word, "Quiet, be still".

I was tempted to put in as a quip, "If only Jesus had been at Chicago Airport!" But, as they say, be careful what you wish for. Ch. 4 ends with, "[The disciples] were terrified and asked each other, 'Who is this? Even the wind and the waves obey him.' " They'd been afraid of the storm but now, amid the calm, they're terrified. The original Greek word is *phobeō*. Another translation could be "they were awestruck" or how about "they had the fear of God."

"Who is Aslan?" asked Susan ...

"Is–is he a man?" asked Lucy.

"Aslan a man!" said Mr Beaver sternly. "Certainly not. I tell you he is the King of the wood and the son of the great Emperor-beyond-the-Sea. Don't you know who is the King of Beasts? Aslan is a lion — the Lion, the great Lion."

"Ooh!" said Susan, "I'd thought he was a man. Is he — quite safe? I shall feel rather nervous about meeting a lion."

"That you will, dearie, and no mistake," said Mrs Beaver; "if there's anyone who can appear before Aslan without their knees knocking, they're either braver than most or else just silly."

"Then he isn't safe?" said Lucy.

"Safe?" said Mr Beaver; "don't you hear what Mrs Beaver tells you? Who said anything about safe? 'Course he isn't safe. But he's good. He's the King, I tell you."

"I'm longing to see him," said Peter, "even if I do feel frightened when it comes to the point."[i]

My only experience with lions has been from behind bars. I did encounter a mountain lion or cougar in Yosemite National Park. Stand your ground, had been the advice given for such an occurrence: I went and hid behind a bush. A herd of elephants in South Africa had been bad enough. We were in what at that moment felt to me to be a very small and flimsy rental car as the herd advanced toward us. My school-friend was leaning out of the driver's window taking photographs. "Brian, they're getting close. Brian!" "OK," said Brian, as he reluctantly wound up the window and reversed off the track.

As we began this sermon series working through Mark's Gospel account, I referred to the iconography traditionally associated with it, a lion. The lion Aslan is C.S. Lewis's way of depicting Jesus in his book *The Lion, the Witch and the Wardrobe*.

P. 973 in the pew Bibles, Mk. ch. 5, v. 15: "When they came to Jesus, they saw the man who had been possessed by the legion of demons, sitting there, dressed and in his right mind, and they were afraid."

In this case, the Greek word is *ephobēthēsan*, which again could be translated as "they were awestruck." No doubt there are sermons which criticise the people for being awestruck. I'm not going to do so because in their place I think I would have been awestruck. I might even have looked around to see if there was a convenient bush! But even with the bush between us, I and the mountain lion were in each other's presence. I remained in the spot to which I had retreated, he looking at me and me at him, transfixed by his presence.

"Who is this?" the disciples asked. I think they were transfixed, awestruck, because they knew what the answer must be. They knew the implication of being in the presence of one whom even the wind and waves obeyed. The man with the evil spirit recognised Jesus for who he was: v. 7, "What do you want with me, Jesus, Son of the Most High God?" After his restoration, v. 18, "the man who had been demon-possessed begged to go with him. Jesus did not let him, but said, 'Go home to your family and tell them how much the Lord has done for you, and how he has had mercy on you.' " How much the Lord — God — has done for you. How did the man interpret this? V. 20, "the man went away and began to tell in the Decapolis how much Jesus had done for him." He knew the implication of what had occurred: Jesus was the Lord, Jesus was God.

In addition to these, what I think are explicit references to who Jesus is and what was transpiring, Mark provides information which I think would have blared to his Jewish audience but perhaps needs unpacking for us. To where were the demons consigned? Pigs, to the Jews, unclean animals. Their loss said that the man's health was worth more than a valuable economic resource: there were two thousand of them.

But what exactly happened to them? V. 13, "[they] rushed down into the lake and were drowned." With what event in the history of Israel would this have resonated? Ex. 14:28: "The water flowed back and covered the chariots and horsemen, the entire army of Pharaoh that had followed the Israelites into the sea. Not one of them survived. But the Israelites went through the sea on dry ground." Who had consigned Pharaoh's army to the sea? God, just as Jesus now did to the demon-infested pigs.

In his vision of the future in Rev. ch. 21 John writes, "Then I saw a new heaven and a new earth, for the first heaven and the first earth had passed away, and there was no longer any sea." Why no sea? Because of its association with evil that was to be done away with.

The effect and power of the storm had been evident. Ch. 4, v. 37, "the waves broke over the boat so that it was nearly swamped." The disciples said to Jesus, "Don't you care if we drown?" [v. 38]. So too, the reality of the presence and power of evil was evident in the man with an evil spirit. V. 3 of our passage: "This man lived in the tombs." His spiritual state was the equivalent of the living dead, a dead man walking. "No one could bind him any more, not even with a chain." No mere human intervention could save him.

As I said, I'd be interested to hear a Unitarian sermon on this passage, because to me, and I hope to you, it speaks clearly of the divinity of Jesus, something Unitarians deny. And it also speaks of the reality of evil and the necessity of divine intervention, in the form of Jesus, to save us from it. Something, again, which Unitarians deny.

Frank Lloyd Wright wrote of Unity Temple: "Why not, then, build a temple, not to God ... but build a temple to man, appropriate to his uses as a meeting place, in which to study man himself for his God's sake? A modern meeting-house and a good-time place."

He is best known for his domestic architecture. The Prairie style of architecture he developed has an emphasis on the horizontal, part reflective of the Midwestern landscape, influenced by his interest in things Japanese. But also reflective of his dismissal of belief in a God who intervenes, who is to be found outside ourselves and our environment. His Unity Temple reflects a domestication of God. The God of which it speaks is indeed safe. Who need be terrified of such a comfortable God of our own making?

The man with an evil spirit presents an obvious and extreme example of the reality of evil in our lives. Interestingly, accoladed architect that he was, Frank Lloyd Wright's personal life was not without its twists and turns. He abandoned his wife and six children to take off with his mistress. Tragedy struck in 1914 when an employee set fire to Wright's new home and killed his mistress and six others. In 1925, the home again burnt down.

Wright's interpretation of the fact that on both occasions his home was burnt, but his studio saved, was that God felt there was something awry in his character as a man but not as an architect.

We read that the man who had been demon-possessed "went away and began to tell all the Decapolis how much Jesus had done for him" [v. 20]. The clue to the nature of the area is in its name, *Decapolis* being Greek for "ten cities". It was a Greek area and Greek culture represented a pinnacle of intellectual and philosophical sophistication. This influence is felt to this day. I think it is seen in the philosophy underpinning Unitarianism. It's no coincidence, I think, that Unity Temple is located in Oak Park, a 'nice' area of Chicago.

I acknowledge that Greek philosophical influence in my background, my education and upbringing: I enjoy the good things that life has to offer, including music and art and architecture. But I recognise that which is awry in my own life, and my need of salvation by God who is beyond such things.

How was the man and his message received? We're told nothing beyond the fact that, v. 20, "all the people were amazed." But we were told in v. 17: "Then the people began to plead with Jesus to leave their region."

Today we baptise Tula. Baptism speaks to us of our need of Jesus in our lives. A passing from darkness into light. Recalling how the Israelites passed through the Red Sea en route to the Promised Land. We will help and encourage Tula to embrace for herself in due course the faith into which she is baptised. Just as we too must do so.

Amen.

Mark 5:21–43, July 13th, 2014

Our passage begins at v. 21 of Mk. ch. 5, p. 973 in the pew Bibles: "When Jesus had again crossed over by boat to the other side of the lake, a large crowd gathered around him while he was by the lake." I like to Internet-surf, seeing where it gets me. I've come across videos of atheists such as Christopher Hitchens and Richard Dawkins peddling their wares. Perhaps my tenderness is owing not only to last week's tooth extraction but also to a sense of being somewhat got at by them!

I found it inspirational to visit the Holy Land in 2007. Highlights were visiting Jerusalem and Lake Galilee, sometimes referred to as a sea: I guess it's too big to be a lake and too small to be a sea! It's the lake that Jesus has been crisscrossing, and yes, it does have storms like the one at the end of ch. 4.

If you're an atheist, you've got to decide how much you don't believe. Few would say that Jesus didn't exist, there's too much evidence that he did. And we've got accounts of what he did and where things took place. I found it inspirational to be in those places. We may be told that there's no evidence for Christianity. Actually, there's a lot of evidence: what Mark writes is part of that. The question is, what do you make of the evidence, how do you respond to it?

Two weeks ago we were on the lake and Jesus demonstrated his power by quelling a storm: "Even the wind and the waves obey him!" [Mk. 4:41]. Last week, on the right side of the lake, the issue was demon-possession; Jesus demonstrated his power by healing the man with an evil spirit. Today, we're on the other side of the lake and the NIV Bible gives us the heading, "A Dead Girl and a Sick Woman."

On the prayer list you'll see we're to pray for Sean in his capacity as 'signmaster': I think we'll have to get him a badge that labels him as such! I presume that our prayers should extend to praying that the sign does what it's supposed to: I hope you've all seen it. It enables us to broadcast a message. We considered 'A Dead Girl and a Sick Woman'. "Attention-grabbing" thought Margaret; "But is it appealing?" thought Sean.

Can anyone tell me what we ended up with? 'Salvation healing through relationship with Jesus.' I don't usually go in for sermon titles, but you've got one this week. Logistics mean that this will probably be the sign's message for a while. But I hope that having a title for this week's sermon helps you and keeps me on track! 'Salvation healing through relationship with Jesus.'

There are two contrasting characters in today's passage who compete for Jesus' attention. One is a person of social standing. He's a man; I'm sorry, but in that setting, that counted for something. He's given a name, Jairus. And he's a synagogue ruler. And he has an urgent need: "My little daughter is dying", v. 23.

The other is a woman: we're not told her name. She had an ongoing need: she "had been subject to bleeding for twelve years", v. 25. We're not told the precise nature of her illness, but the assumption is that it's related to her being a woman. And it would have added to her exclusion: physically, religiously and socially. See Lev. 15 for details of how the Jewish system regarded her: she was unclean. This is why, rather than coming before Jesus and addressing him, she feels able only to come up behind him in a crowd and touch his cloak, v. 27.

If you go on a time-management course, you may be told to draw four boxes and label them: urgent and important; non-urgent and important; urgent and unimportant; non-urgent and unimportant. This is supposed to help you prioritise tasks and make sure things get done. The box I most struggle with is non-urgent yet important: the urgent generally seems to take over, even if it's relatively unimportant: the tyranny of the urgent.

Jesus is going with Jairus, having acceded to his request for help, which I think may be placed in the urgent and important box: his daughter is dying. Things so far are going as well as they can from Jairus' point of view. We can imagine him trying to make a way for Jesus through the crowd. But then things start going awry.

Jesus encounters the woman and Jairus seemingly disappears from view. If I were he, I think I'd be hopping from foot to foot, my face desperately telegraphing my feelings at this point.

How would we view the woman's situation? Perhaps, important but non-urgent. After all, it had been going on for twelve years. I'm afraid that some of her day would have regarded her as both non-urgent and unimportant. Jesus doesn't.

It takes only an instant for the woman to be healed. V. 29 begins with a characteristic Mark word: "Immediately". But Jesus stops, turns around, addresses the crowd and talks to the woman.

The encounter illustrates Jesus' power and also the self-imposed limitations of his then ministry. Jesus knows something has occurred because he realises, v. 30, "that power has gone out of him." But to find out more, he has to resort to a question: "Who touched my clothes?" The fact that power went out from him speaks of the personal cost of his ministry. We gain at his expense.

We don't know how long the encounter took: Mark devotes ten verses to it. But it's long enough for the news to arrive that Jairus's daughter has died. Perhaps Jairus would have agreed to the question, "Why bother the teacher any more?", v. 35. And also thought, 'If only.' If only that woman hadn't been there. If only Jesus had got his priorities right.

Richard Dawkins says he isn't interested in 'why' questions. He regards them as unscientific. But nonetheless, they are natural ones for us to ask. They are sometimes asked with regard to prayer. Part of my response is to refer to what we know as the Prayer of St. Chrysostom: "Fulfil now, O Lord, the desires and petitions of thy servants, as may be most expedient for them."

I hope it's not seen as an avoidance of a 'why' question to direct you to the purposes of God for an answer. Is. 55:8: " 'my thoughts are not your thoughts, neither are your ways my ways,' declares the Lord." And God's ability to bring good out of bad. A key verse, which I hope does not become trite through overuse, is

Rom. 8:28: "we know that in all things God works for the good of those who love him."

Jesus ignores the suggestion that there's no more to be done regarding Jairus's daughter and proceeds to the home. He goes in and says, "The child is not dead but asleep", v. 39. In response, "they laughed at him." If you've ever been laughed at, take heart, it's happened to Jesus.

Was Jairus's daughter dead? In one sense, I'm in no doubt that she was. That's what caused the mourners to laugh at him. They were likely to be professional mourners, they knew when someone was dead.

It's becoming commonplace to refer euphemistically to death. When letting agencies know of the death of my mother, I would be asked 'when she passed'. But to refer to someone who has died as sleeping can be an accurate expression of what we believe about them and the Christian hope. The etymology of the word cemetery is 'sleeping place'. Paul refers to people who have died as "those who have fallen asleep." I Thess. 4:14: "We believe that Jesus died and rose again and so we believe that God will bring with Jesus those who have fallen asleep in him."

Paul is talking about the return of Jesus, the Second Coming. But Jesus is already present at Jairus's house. In this case, it is all the more relevant to refer to death as sleep, as we see enacted a precursor of what will happen at the General Resurrection following Jesus' return.

V. 41, "[Jesus] took her by the hand and said to her, '*Talitha koum*!' (which means, 'Little girl, I say to you, get up!'). Immediately the girl stood up and walked around."

In ch. 4, Jesus' power over nature had been demonstrated through the quelling of the storm. We've seen his power at work against demons in the restoration of the man with an evil spirit. Now the adversary is death itself. Again, Jesus' power is demonstrated.

When the woman who had been subject to bleeding fell at Jesus' feet, she was "trembling with fear", v. 33. Jesus tells her to "Go in peace" [v. 34]. Jesus tells Jairus, v. 36, "Don't be afraid." Death and sickness can be a source of fear. But these accounts assure us that Jesus' power is more than a match for anything we face. We can claim the peace that Jesus brings through faith in him and his power to overcome. "Daughter, your faith has healed you." "Don't be afraid; just believe."

How was the woman's faith in Jesus expressed? V. 28, "she thought, 'If I just touch his clothes (the only thing she felt capable of in her desperate situation), I will be healed.' " The woman was seeking healing and that is what she received: v. 29, "Immediately her bleeding stopped and she felt in her body that she was freed from her suffering."

She sought and received physical healing. Along with this would come restoration from the ostracism her illness brought. But also, through Jesus' response to what had occurred, she now finds herself at his feet, receiving his word of peace. The Greek word translated 'healed' also means 'saved'. She received healing and restoration. But also a new relationship between her and Jesus that speaks of a greater salvation.

Jesus went with Jairus. He went in where the child was. He took her by the hand. And the literal meaning of the Aramaic word he uses to address her is 'little lamb', 'get up little lamb'. By such a touch and words, a twelve-year-old had her life restored to her. But it would now be a life that had been touched, literally, by a healer who is also a saviour. To be addressed in such a way on awakening from death is surely to live a new life in relationship with one who both heals and saves.

These are precious instances that Mark has recorded for us. Our sharing in the experience of the woman, Jairus and his daughter must in one sense be vicarious, at second hand. Before you begrudge them that experience, remember the suffering out of which it came: twelve years of bleeding; the pain of separation through death.

These events occurred for the benefit of those involved. But they also occurred, and are recorded by Mark, for our benefit. Yes, so that we may share in the joy of those who were there. But also that we might enter into relationship with Jesus, who offers us healing and salvation through his healing and saving power.

Amen.

Mark 6:1–29, July 20th, 2014

I mentioned last week that the account Mark gives us of Jesus' ministry is part of the evidence that we have about it. It contains details which we can see as authenticating. We've heard about Jesus crisscrossing Lake Galilee. Now he heads for his home town, Nazareth, another place you can visit if you visit the Holy Land.

Up until now, things have been going pretty well. We can feel we have been backing a winner in Jesus. OK, the people of the region of the Gerasenes had pleaded with Jesus to leave their region, ch. 5, v. 17, but that was in reaction to his success in dealing with a demon-possessed man, and we can say more fool they.

This is the sort of Jesus some people like. I was fascinated to visit a Protestant church in Berlin; it was built between 1933 and 1935 and represented Christianity that had allowed itself to be hijacked by the Nazis. Aspects of the building were designed to reflect a form of muscular Christianity. My guide pointed out the crucifix and expressed the view that the figure of Jesus was reminiscent of Arnold Schwarzenegger.

In 1925 Pope Pius XI instituted the Feast of Christ the King. One of the motivations was to fight back against the advance of atheistic communism, with a triumphalistic Christian message. And this lay behind the Church's muted response to Nazism. Some felt the Church needed an ally as it faced the threat of Soviet communism. This, of course, was a tragic mistake. As Jesus said to Paul: "My grace is sufficient for you, for my power is made perfect in weakness", II Cor. 12:9.

There's a temptation to hanker for the success of the Church. I confess how I fell prey to this desire when in my salad days. Friends, God does not call for a successful Church. What does he call for? What does he call us to be? He calls us to be faithful.

Ch. 6 brings us down with a bump. The people of Jesus' home town said of him, v. 3, "Isn't this the carpenter? ... And they took offence at him." I call this prejudice. What is it based on? He's only a carpenter, not very impressive. And look at the family he comes from. No matter that he's got wisdom, even miracles. In this instance, it isn't that he isn't one of us; in fact that's the problem; he probably speaks with a local accent. Not very impressive. It's a case of shoot the messenger, in spite of his message.

I recently learnt the contemporary meaning of the word hipster. I always thought that hipster meant a type of underwear. But apparently it means someone who is an effortlessly cool urban bohemian: I looked that one up. Having learnt this, I have visions of someone, somewhere, not to do with Holy Trinity of course, advocating that the Church go for the hipster market, by hipsterising the Church. Don't get me wrong: I've got nothing against hipsters, in either sense of the word. And if you're a hipster who's a Christian, good on ya. Keep on being authentically hipsterish.

The danger for the Church, however, is twofold. People who self-evidently aren't hipsters, trying to pretend that they are. Inauthenticity is quickly seen through. And more dangerously, people acting like the young child who's more interested in the wrapping paper than the gift. Jesus was authentic to who he was. Yes, a carpenter, a local lad from a local family. What mattered though, was his message. He preached it and it was rejected. We are called to proclaim the same message. And not to be surprised if it's rejected. It happened to Jesus and it will happen to us.

The people of Nazareth said something significant, probably without realising it. V. 2: "What's this wisdom that has been given to him?" Real wisdom comes from God. Paul speaks of Jesus, the Nazareth carpenter, as being, "the power of God and the wisdom of God", I Cor. 1:24. But there are two caveats. This is the Jesus who is Christ crucified; which, counterculturally, is where power and wisdom is focussed. In Jesus, as the one who was willing to die for us. And secondly, it is those whom God has called, who are able to see Jesus this way. Faith itself is a gift from God.

In our quest for success, we can take our eye off the ball. Can forget what we're meant to be about; where true, God-given wisdom and power is to be found. Can think instead that the trappings, the packaging, are what matters and will win people round. Jesus' searing indictment of the people of Nazareth in v. 6 is, "he was amazed by their lack of faith." We must always ask ourselves whether we have the Christ-centred faithfulness that God looks for.

An aspect of the dismissal of Jesus by the people of Nazareth is the fact that familiarity can breed contempt. This explains the rise in popularity of novel religious expressions, such as the allure of Eastern religions. Christianity, and in particular, established expressions of it such as Anglicanism, can appear to be old hat: the religion of our parents or grandparents. In the face of this, there's all the more need for us to demonstrate the relevance of the old, old story of Jesus and his love.

If Mark had had a publisher looking over his shoulder when writing his gospel account, then the publisher might have questioned the inclusion of the last part of our passage, vv. 14–29. It's a break in the narrative flow: looking back to an event that occurred earlier. The publisher might have argued: you've entitled your work, good news; what's good about your section, John the Baptist Beheaded? And he would have a point. Speak out for what's right, and what happens? Your head may end up on a platter. Not exactly good Sunday school material.

Gospel is usually translated as good news. But whether you regard the gospel as good news depends on your point of view; how you respond to it. For it also contains a word of judgement, regarding our condition and actions outside of a saving faith in Christ.

John the Baptist had spoken such a word of judgement to Herod; and it had some effect on him. V. 20: "Herod feared John and protected him, knowing him to be a righteous and holy man. When Herod heard John, he was greatly puzzled; yet he liked to listen to him." But eventually, it was the world that held sway over Herod. There was Herodias, his wife, who nursed a grudge against John and wanted to kill him. Quite a grudge, v. 19. And Herodias's daughter, who was evidently quite a dancer.

In the heat of the moment, Herod makes a rash promise. V. 22: "Ask me for anything you want, and I'll give it to you." Herod was greatly distressed by the girl's request, v. 25, "Give me right now the head of John the Baptist on a platter." But his distress, and the fact that he knew John "to be a righteous and holy man", didn't amount to much, in the face of his oaths and his dinner guests, v. 26. We're back to what matters more: the ways of the world, vested interest and power, keeping up appearances, or God's way and following God's will?

May I introduce you to a theological word? Pericope. It's a posh word for a set of Bible verses that form one coherent unit of thought. You can dazzle someone now, with the fact that today's reading in church contains three pericopes. We've looked at two so far: Jesus' rejection in Nazareth, at the beginning of the passage, and John's beheading at the end of the passage. So, by deduction, the third pericope we're going to look at is the bit in between: Jesus' sending out of the twelve disciples.

Now perhaps, when hearing the passage read, you thought, what a strange mixture of stories; what is the connection between them? I hope that this may be becoming clearer. Jesus had been rejected by the people of Nazareth. John had been rejected by Herod, to the point that he forfeited his life. And Jesus predicts to the twelve disciples that they also are likely to be rejected, v. 11: "if any place will not welcome you or listen to you, shake the dust off your feet when you leave as a testimony against them."

It's significant that Jesus' response to his rejection is to send his disciples out, to preach that people should repent, v. 12, and to do so in the knowledge that they too are likely to suffer rejection. And Mark indicates the extreme form that that rejection could take, in the example of what happened to John. John had been the forerunner before Jesus' ministry began and now John's death prefigures Jesus' betrayal and death, in which Herod, again, was to play a part.

The message is, don't expect being a follower of Jesus to be a path of unmitigated success. You should expect opposition. The world, with its pressures, expectations, temptations and demands is ever near. In fact, the anti-success message in this passage is so strong, I would go so far as to ask: if we're not experiencing opposition, are we doing what Jesus wants in terms of following him?

It can be tempting to water down the gospel in order to make it more attractive, that we might have success. How about a prosperity gospel that promises riches? Or a Jesus of love who doesn't care about right and wrong?

I watched a television debate between the atheist Richard Dawkins and Cardinal George Pell of Sydney. All credit to the cardinal for being willing to be put on the spot in that way. He said some things that were good and helpful and true. But I also found myself shaking my head, as he said things that, to my mind, compromised the gospel, albeit in the face of a potentially hostile studio audience. In emphasising a God of love and unconditional acceptance, at times I felt that he lost sight of Jesus as the Bible presents him to us.

Are we faithful to Jesus in the way we present him? Is the gospel message we proclaim, one centred on Christ crucified? A gospel of power made perfect in weakness. Are we willing to face rejection for the sake of Jesus and the gospel?

> O Jesus, I have promised
>   To serve thee to the end;
> Be Thou forever near me,
>   My master and my friend!
> I shall not fear the battle
>   If Thou art by my side,
> Nor wander from the pathway
>   If thou wilt be my guide.

Oh, let me see thy footprints,
  And in them plant my own!
My hope to follow duly
  Is in thy strength alone,
Oh, guide me, call me, draw me,
  Uphold me to the end!
And then in heaven receive me,
  My saviour and my friend!

          Amen.

Mark 6:30–44, October 5th, 2014

We return to our sermon series looking at Mark's gospel account. The idea behind working our way progressively through Bible books is that we get a chance to look at a book as a whole, if only bit by bit. Seeing it as the author intended, as it was written. We have had a break, leaving off at v. 29 of ch. 6 at the end of July. That's a reason for having your Bibles open, so you can see what's happened before. So may I encourage you to do so, p. 974 in the church Bibles.

The two previous passages are headed in the New International Version, 'John the Baptist Beheaded' and 'Jesus Sends Out the Twelve'. Both of these passages are of relevance to what we're going to look at today.

First, what happened to John was in the context of a banquet Herod threw for, v. 21, "his officials and military commanders and the leading men of Galilee." There's a contrast between who Herod was, a puppet king installed by the Romans, and the type of banquet he presided over, and who Jesus was, a king with the power and authority of God, and the type of banquet over which he is to preside.

And the Sending Out of the Twelve links in with the first verse of our passage, v. 30, "The apostles gathered around Jesus and reported to him all they had done and taught." We read at v. 12 that "They went out and preached that people should repent. They drove out many demons and [healed] many sick people." A combination of preaching/teaching and action: the two go together.

Mission is, happily, in vogue nowadays, both inside and outside the Church: witness the businesses that have adopted 'mission statements'. But there's a danger in overusing the term just as there is in losing sight of it. The word 'mission' means 'sending'. It isn't mission if we're just talking about something inside the Church; it's got to be related to those who are outside.

Having gone out and preached and acted, "The apostles gathered around Jesus and reported to him". This is embryonic evidence of the Church having structure and people being responsible to others for what they do, in this case the apostles being responsible to Jesus. This is entirely right and proper, although I fear that our form-filling and box-ticking culture can sometimes take it to extremes.

The apostles would no doubt have been looking for encouragement from Jesus: the basis of appraisal should be praise. And they would have been tired after all their activity. There's a hymn that's criticised because it describes Jesus as "Lone and dreary, faint and weary": does anyone know what that hymn is? (It's 'Lead us, heavenly Father, lead us'.) I think the problem is that people don't like thinking of Jesus as "dreary". Leaving that aside, I think that Jesus, in his humanity, did get faint and weary and that enables him to relate to us when we too get weary.

The film *Chariots of Fire* set at the 1924 Olympics was revived at the time of the London Olympics in 2012. I remember it the first time round. It is 1982 and I was in my first week as a student at Durham. St. Nicholas' Church had a screening on the Saturday. And we watched the character Eric Liddell, a Christian athlete who wouldn't compete on Sundays, reading from the Book of Isaiah at the Church of Scotland church in Paris: "Even youths grow tired and weary", an affirmation that even those engaged in Christian ministry, as I hope we all are, can grow weary. The passage continues, "but those who hope in the Lord will renew their strength" and then, and this was particularly apposite for the film, "They will soar on wings like eagles; they will run and not grow weary", although, speaking personally, I feel that this is more a vision of what is to come.

Jesus, as the sensitive leader, recognising the disciples' condition and in the light of there being "so many people ... coming and going that they did not have a chance to eat", v. 31 of our passage, says to the apostles, "Come with me by yourselves to a quiet place and get some rest."

They got there. I don't know how much time they had to rest; they travelled by boat so perhaps that was an opportunity. Meanwhile, v. 33, "Many ... ran on foot from all the towns and got there ahead of them". I wonder how the apostles felt about that: I can imagine how I might have felt had I been one of them: 'Come on, give us a break!'

V. 34, "Jesus landed and saw a large crowd." What was his reaction? I've already mentioned his sensitivity to the apostles' needs. And his plan to meet that by going to a quiet place was being scuppered by the appearance of the crowd. But there's something that must always take precedence in Christian ministry. It's summed up by a wonderful word: compassion. The Greek word for this is special to the New Testament in turning compassion into a verb and in relating it to Christ. It's something only Jesus, as God, can truly have. We can have it as Christians in as much as we share in 'the compassion of Christ'.

Jesus had compassion toward the crowd because he saw "they were like sheep without a shepherd". This harks back to the history of Old Testament Israel. God's people needed a shepherd to lead them. This rôle was fulfilled by various people: Moses who then appointed Joshua. The greatest shepherd of Israel was King David, but even his reign didn't end well. By the time of the prophet Ezekiel things were in a sorry state and this leads the Lord to say, "I myself will search for my sheep and look after them", Ez. 34:11. And this is what God does in the form of his Son, Jesus.

I've come across what I think is a false dichotomy between being pastoral and teaching. The way that Jesus shepherds is by "teaching them many things." Teaching is at the heart of pastoral ministry. We don't know for how long Jesus taught. I recall the Dean of Durham telling me that the cathedral's congregation could manage only ten-minute sermons. I suspect that Jesus went on for longer than that: he taught them "many things" and, v. 35, "By this time it was late in the day."

The disciples, earlier referred to as apostles, came to Jesus and said, v. 36, "Send the people away so they can go to the surrounding countryside and villages and buy themselves something to eat." You can see the way the disciples were thinking: "so they can go ... and buy themselves something to eat", an emphasis on 'they' and 'them'. Jesus bats back, v. 37, with an emphasis on 'you': "You give them something to eat."

The obvious way of doing this would be from what the disciples already had, which we discover was five loaves and two fish. But the disciples assume that this can't be what Jesus means: first, they want the supper for themselves and second, it wouldn't go very far among 5,000, or so they assume. But you know what assuming does: it makes an 'ass' out of 'u' and 'me'.

They've heard what God, in Jesus, has said to them, and they turn it into something rational that makes sense to them and serve it back with a dose of sarcasm: "Are we to go and spend that much on bread and give it them to eat?" If God tells us to jump, what should our response be? To do so. But, if you're minded to talk back, "How high?" would be OK.

You know what happened. You've heard the account read, as I suspect you've heard it before, perhaps as far back as Sunday School. The details add to the authenticity of the miracle. The green grass, groups of hundreds and fifties: there really were that many people there, just as there had been when Moses divided up the Israelites in the wilderness where God provided manna to eat. Jesus presides over the meal, as Herod had over his banquet, but Jesus isn't Herod; he's something far better. He looked up to heaven, gave thanks, broke the loaves and divided the fish.

V. 42: "They all ate and were satisfied, and the disciples picked up twelve basketfuls of broken pieces of bread and fish." Jesus is Lord of all creation. Obey him and nothing is impossible. And his gracious provision overflows; in this case to the tune of twelve basketfuls.

For whose benefit was this miracle performed? Yes, all who were there benefitted as they got what they needed: "They all ate and were satisfied". But I'm surmising that the people didn't know what had happened, beyond the fact that they were fed. They had no reason to know that the disciples had only five loaves and two fish to begin with. But the disciples knew. And we know. What were they and what are we to take away from the passage we've looked at?

The apostles/disciples, at the beginning of our passage, were weary, not to mention hungry. And we too can grow weary, perhaps it's fair to say, are weary. I detect this. Last Wednesday, I was at an excellent event regarding evangelism in the 21st century. It came across how wearing ministry can be, just keeping the existing Church going, yet alone reaching out to others. Diocesan clergy gathered on Thursday and it was the same story, as it has been on other occasions. Jesus understands. But he doesn't let that deflect him from looking outwards. His compassion is directed toward those outside: the sheep without a shepherd.

One of the ironies, I felt, of the evangelism day, was that those responsible for the venue, concerned about the outside door banging, put up a notice asking for it to be closed quietly because "a retreat was in progress." It reminds me of a version of the Parable of the Good Samaritan, which we looked at recently in our Thursday Bible study, where the priest hurries by on the other side, ignoring the man in distress, because he's on his way to a conference on Christian outreach. Friends, we're not called to retreat, but to advance and engage.

The disciples found themselves in a "remote place". This had been intentional. What hadn't been planned was that all these needy people be present. As the immediate need was food, this may be considered about as bad a place to exercise ministry as possible. Vancouver, likewise, I've heard it said many times, can be considered a hard place to minister. The most secular city in North America. But it is where God has placed us, here at Holy Trinity.

"The Church is in crisis. There are difficulties, limitations, insoluble problems, lack of people and money, a menacing outlook, endless misunderstandings and misrepresentations." No, these words aren't taken from the Rector of Holy Trinity's report! The actual quotation, which is from an old commentary on II Corinthians, is "The church is always in a crisis and always will be. There will be difficulties etc." And it continues, "We are not only to do our work despite these things; they are precisely the conditions requisite for the doing of it." "It is not God's intention that we should in ourselves be adequate for our tasks, rather He wants that we should be inadequate" in order that his grace and power may be displayed through us. God says to each one of us, individually and as his Church here at Holy Trinity, as he did to Paul, "My grace is sufficient for you, for my power is made perfect in weakness", II Cor. 12:9.

The disciples learnt through the feeding of the five thousand that nothing is impossible to God. It's good for us spiritually to be up against it in human terms because it's precisely then as we turn to God in prayer, as we admit our need of him, that he can be at work. Not to rationalise, to find a human way out. Rather, we are called to listen to God's Word to us, to trust it and obey.

Last Tuesday, we had the first session of our *Christianity Explored* course. I was heartened by those among us who desired to engage further with Mark's gospel account in this way. But the true value of the course is if it builds us up, empowers us, to be able to share the good news of Jesus Christ with others. This can happen in many ways. And I hope it does. Perhaps you might feel encouraged to join the course, it's not too late to do so. But also to think of someone currently outside the Church whom you could invite. That could be a part in sharing Jesus' compassion toward those outside, engaging in God's mission.

Amen.

Mark 6:45–56, October 19th, 2014

In 1970 Roger Whittaker sang 'I Don't Believe in If Anymore'. What about 'if only'? I get the feeling there're still plenty of 'if onlies' floating about. Either personally: "If only I hadn't done something or said whatever." Or, how about with the Church: "If only we had more people, or more money." And often things seem to hinge on one person. I've heard it said, "We couldn't cope without so-and-so." Friends, no-one is indispensable, apart from one person, who is … ? Jesus.

Some of you kindly completed forms as part of the Natural Church Development process, for which we are very grateful. Individual forms are anonymous: I don't know who completed any particular form. But I couldn't help noticing that someone had qualified one of the answers. The statement on the form that had to be responded to was "I firmly believe that God will work more powerfully in the coming years." The qualification that had been added was, "Not without more people."

Let's have a look at the situation of Jesus and the disciples in our passage; you'll find it on p. 975 of the church Bibles; Mk. ch. 6, beginning at v. 45. First a characteristic Markan word, "Immediately": there's a sense of urgency, there's work to be done. And then the word "made": "Immediately Jesus made his disciples get into the boat and go on ahead of him to Bethsaida." The Greek word the NIV translates as "made" actually justifies a stronger translation: Jesus compelled the disciples to go. Perhaps they were reluctant, let's face it, we tend to like to stay where we are, doing what we're familiar with, but they did as he said.

Then what did Jesus do? V. 46, "he went up on a mountainside to pray." Yes, there was an urgency. But I won't say that it wasn't so urgent that there was time to pray. Because it's when things are most urgent that prayer is most vital. I commend to you the opportunities for prayer in our services, our prayer list for your personal use and our prayer meetings. Prayer must be a priority, especially when other things seem urgent.

About what did Jesus pray? We're not told. But that's not going to stop me from speculating! I think it may have had something to do with what we read at v. 52: "[the disciples] had not understood about the loaves [that is, the Feeding of the Five Thousand, which had occurred immediately before]; their hearts were hardened."

Jesus had only twelve disciples to work with, and one of them was to betray him, so that makes eleven. He was down to a cricket or soccer team! Imagine, a Church of eleven or twelve people: that's what Jesus had to work with, that's whom he was to entrust his mission to. And they didn't understand, their hearts were hardened. So he prayed: prayer is vital. But combine Jesus and prayer and even only eleven people of limited understanding, and God can still work powerfully.

In one of the small groups at *Christianity Explored* last Tuesday, we got into a discussion about the all-seeing eye of God. It was in relation to the question, "Imagine that all your thoughts, words and actions were displayed for everyone to see." Leaving aside how this might, or might not, relate to American bank notes, Jesus saw the disciples struggling, v. 48, "straining at the oars, because the wind was against them." It should be a source of comfort to us that Jesus sees our struggles.

And Jesus acts. The implication is that Jesus had seen the disciples "in the middle of the lake" "when evening came". But it wasn't until "About the fourth watch of the night (that is, 3 a.m.) [that] he went out to them, walking on the lake." Perhaps God's timing isn't always as we would have it. The Bible uses a special Greek word, *kairos*, to refer to the appointed time in the purpose of God, the time when God acts.

If I were to ask you if anything strikes you as strange or curious in our passage, you may say, someone walking on water. But this is Jesus, the one whom the wind and waves obey, the Lord of creation. I take it as read that if Jesus wants to walk on water he can do it and he does it. Indeed, Mark mentions it almost casually:

"he went out to them, walking on the water." Jesus sees the disciples' need, he wants to reach them, so why not walk, it beats swimming!

So if not that, what is the curious bit I'm thinking about? The end of v. 48: "He was about to pass by them." Are we so captivated by the walking on water that we miss this detail or don't give it due consideration? Indeed, the NIV heads our passage "Jesus Walks on the Water", as if this is all that matters. And it's something that for once the NIV Study Bible that I'm so fond of lets us down on: its notes fail to mention it. But to Mark and those who read his gospel account first off, that clause, "He was about to pass by them," would have sounded a great big, clanging bell.

Yes, of course, the fact that Jesus walks on water has significance: it underlines his divinity. Job said of God: "He alone stretches out the heavens and walks on the waves of the sea", Job 9:8. But, having restated Jesus' divinity, Mark then makes a deliberate connection between what's occurring and God's action in the Old Testament.

In the Old Testament, God appeared to Moses and to Elijah. Moses had said to God, "show me your glory", Ex. 33:18. In response, God says, "no one may see me and live." The compromise is that God places Moses in the cleft of a rock and covers him with his hand "until I have passed by." Do you see the connection? "Until I have passed by." Likewise, Elijah is told, "the Lord is about to pass by", I Ki. 19:11.

In our passage, Mark has established Jesus' divinity through the walking on water. And Jesus points to his divinity when he says, "It is I", v. 50, resonant of Ex. 3:14: "God said to Moses, 'I am who I am. This is what you are to say to the Israelites: 'I am has sent me to you.' " But instead of God, in the form of Jesus, passing by, v. 51, "he climbed in the boat with them".

I'm not a great fan of attempts to differentiate between the Old and New Testament with regard to God's actions. You know, the inaccurate cliché of the god of vengeance in the Old Testament and the god of love in the New: it simply isn't true. The heretic Marcion took it to extremes in the second century by saying there were two different gods for the two testaments. There are not!

There is however, a significant difference between the Old Testament and the New in the way that God relates to his people. The New Testament testifies to God Incarnate, God taking on human flesh: Jesus. Moses hides in the cleft of a rock and is shielded by God's hand; Elijah is in a cave and "pulled his cloak over his face" because "no one may see [God] and live." We don't need to hide in a rock or cave to shield us from our encounter with God. When Augustus Montague Toplady wrote in his hymn, "Rock of ages, cleft for me, let me hide myself in thee", he was speaking metaphorically. The rock to which he refers is Jesus, God revealed to us, to encounter and relate to as one of us.

As Christians our "life is now hidden with Christ in God", Col. 3:3. This is the God who says to the disciples, "Take courage! It is I. Don't be afraid." This is the God who, v. 51, "climbed into the boat with them, and the wind died down." God was in the same boat as the disciples, literally. When he was with them, the wind that had been buffeting them died down. And they were amazed.

Matthew Henry wrote in the early eighteenth century: "The church is often like a ship at sea, tossed with tempests, and not comforted: we may have Christ for us, yet wind and tide against us; but it is a comfort to Christ's disciples in a storm, that their Master is in the heavenly mount, interceding for them. And no difficulties can hinder Christ's appearance for his people, when the set time is come. He silenced their fears, by making himself known to them. Our fears are soon satisfied, if our mistakes are set right, especially our mistakes as to Christ. Let the disciples have their Master with them, and all is well."

Jesus sees our struggles, personally and together as a Church, just as he saw the disciples struggling. He entrusts his mission to us, sending us out, not in spite of who we are: few in number, lacking resources, even understanding, the "if onlies" that might hold us back; but because of who we are and where he has placed us, as part of his Church here at Holy Trinity. Friends, if we are his, if we believe that Jesus is with us in the boat, we are rich indeed; his grace abounds and overflows: our life protected from any storms that assail us, for we are "hidden with Christ in God."

Jesus does not leave us alone, for he is in the boat that is his Church with us. The biggest issue that faces us is not lack of money or people. It's whether we believe that having Christ with us makes the crucial difference. That his touch has still its ancient power. That God can and will work powerfully, for in Christ he is with us still.

Amen.

Mark 7:1–23, November 12th, 2017

I attended a primary school that really couldn't have been any closer to where I lived. My home was in a cul-de-sac, at the end of which was the school. Admittedly, you couldn't get out at that end, so you had to go to the other end, then round the corner and down the school drive.

Because of this proximity, I used to walk home for lunch. Then my mother decided she would get a job. She chose one that allowed her to see me off in the morning, and she was home before I was in the afternoon. But I would have to stay at school for lunch. Oh dear, my mother didn't love me any more; I considered ringing child services to let them know of such wanton neglect and abuse.

Needless to say, I soon adjusted to the new regime. Part of which involved showing your hands to the 'dinner ladies' as you entered the dining hall. If your hands weren't considered clean enough, you'd be sent back to wash them. I learnt a trick: pass your hands under the tap and don't dry them. Wet hands were sure to get you past inspection.

The Pharisees were unlike the dinner ladies in that they were not concerned about matters of hygiene. They weren't the sort of people who put up the notices we see in restaurant washrooms; "Employees must wash their hands" makes me wonder, what about the rest of us? We had Polish relatives visiting us, who were intrigued by a notice they read as "No wash your hands": they hadn't recognised the significance of the 'w'! "Now wash your hands."

But the Pharisees did have something in common with young Karl's approach to pre-dining handwashing. What they required was akin to his quick pass of the hands under the tap: of no particular use other than giving evidence, in my case misleading evidence, that a requirement had been met.

It was this that Jesus' disciples weren't doing. I came across an example of this when I visited India. We persuaded our guide, somewhat reluctantly, to take us to a Christian church. Afterwards, before recommencing our tour, he went to a tap in the street and washed his hands. He considered himself to have been made unclean through entering a church. I felt vaguely offended by this; fortunately, he didn't feel the need to do the same every time he made contact with us.

Jesus takes the Pharisees head-on about all this. When dealing with the common people he could be gentle Jesus, meek and mild; but when confronting their leaders, people he considered should know better, and who were leading others astray, he tended to take no prisoners.

Please turn to our passage, which you'll find on p. 975 of the church Bibles, Mk. ch. 7.

V. 6: "Isaiah was right when he prophesied about you hypocrites." Ouch. That would be enough nowadays to make Jesus a candidate for self-awareness training: "Mr. Christ, or may I call you Jesus, we're not sure that you're fully aware of the impact of you words and actions on others: people are concerned."

Jesus continues regardless: one might as well be hanged for a sheep as a lamb. "These people honour me with their lips, but their hearts are far from me. They worship me in vain; their teachings are but rules taught by men."

Jesus is not against saying things with our lips as part of worship. He's not against hymns, spoken prayers, even ones from a book, or reciting creeds etc. He's not forbidding all religious ceremonies. However, such words are not pleasing to God unless they are a true expression of our hearts, and a distillation of what's been going on in our hearts all week. Too much of religious observance is ritual without reality; outward form without power; lips without heart.

V. 8: " 'You have let go of the commands of God and are holding on to the traditions of men.' And he said to them, 'You have a fine way of setting aside the commands of God in order to observe your own traditions!' " V. 13: "you nullify the word of God by your tradition."

Three times, Jesus says the same thing, a sure sign that we need to take note. The "traditions of men" are contrasted with "the word of God". The Pharisees had allowed their traditions to smother the word of God. This is what the Reformation was all about; this is what Martin Luther railed against.

As a Reformation Church, we hold that Scripture has supreme authority over the traditions of the Church and individuals. "The doctrine of the Church of England is grounded in the Holy Scriptures", Canon A5 of the Church of England. "Holy Scripture containeth all things necessary to salvation", Article VI of the Articles of Religion.

Jesus gives a practical example. V. 11: "you say that if a man says to his father or mother: 'Whatever help you might otherwise have received from me is Corban' (that is, a gift devoted to God), then you no longer let him do anything for his father or mother."

We began our service with the Ten Commandments, including Commandment Six: "Honour thy father and thy mother", one my parents were fond of quoting at me. One of the implications of this Commandment is that if our parents are in physical need, and we're in a position to do something to help them out, then we should.

But some of these Pharisees, it seems, weren't too keen on having to pay for the upkeep of their parents. So they used a loop-hole in the Law to avoid their responsibilities. The system was this: if you had a lump of money in your savings account, you could nominate it as 'Corban' as they called it, in other words as a gift devoted to God, without actually having to give it away. Then, because it was so-called devoted to God, you weren't allowed to give it away to anyone else, not even to your parents.

The money would stay safely stashed away in their accounts, while their parents went short, or someone else had to step in to look after them. By means of this traditional rule, they got to look spiritual, apparently dedicating this money to God, while actually just being miserly at the expense of their parents, and at the expense of obedience to the word of God.

V. 20: Jesus said, "What comes out of a man is what makes him 'unclean.' For from within, out of men's hearts, come evil thoughts, sexual immorality, theft, murder, adultery, greed, malice, deceit, lewdness, envy, slander, arrogance and folly. All these evils come from inside and make a man 'unclean.' "

Jesus says that moral purity is much more important than ceremonial purity. What makes people unclean in God's sight is the evil that emanates from their heart.

The Swiss Reformer John Calvin spoke of "the total depravity of man." By this, he didn't mean that we are all totally depraved. We know, as did he, that there are evident differences in the extent to which evil has hold of people. What Calvin was getting at is the fact that none of us is immune from the grip of evil, and this affects, to some extent or other, every aspect of our lives. "If we say that we have no sin, we deceive ourselves, and the truth is not in us", I Jn. 1:8 [AV]; "all have sinned and fall short of the glory of God", Rom. 3:23.

Jesus did not teach the fundamental goodness of human nature. The extent of human evil is universal. Jesus isn't referring just to some criminal element, but to the Pharisees, those who were considered religious and righteous. We need to be careful if we seek to demonise a particular person or group; remember, there but for the grace of God go I.

All of the examples Jesus gives of what makes us unclean in God's eyes are outworkings of our basic self-centredness. Sin means me first, my neighbour next, when it suits me, and God somewhere off in the distance.

English is rich with words compounded with the prefix self, so many of them negative: self-advertisement, -applause, -gratification, -glorification, -indulgence, self-will, self-pity, and so on. We need this rich vocabulary, in order to describe these manifestations of our basic evil that defiles us and makes us unfit to be in God's presence.

We've looked at worship: is it with the heart or only from the lips, paying lip-service. Authority: do we stand on Scripture and Scripture alone, over and above any manmade tradition. Morality: do we seek inward purity, rather than mere outward appearance. We need to ask ourselves, in each of these areas, whose side are we on, that of the Pharisees, or that of Jesus.

We need to be washed clean and we need a new heart, and that is what the gospel offers us. We need the good news of Jesus Christ. He died for our sins, bearing them in his innocent person on the cross, in order that we may be forgiven, and washed clean in God's sight.

He who so died for us, rose again and is alive, and by his Holy Spirit can enter into our personality and change us from within; giving us a new heart, with new desires, ambitions and aspirations.

These two things together, Jesus' death and resurrection, cleansing, giving us a new heart for God, constitute the new beginning, the new life, that is offered to us in the gospel. Don't miss it. Embrace it today, by accepting Jesus as your personal Lord and Saviour.

Amen.

Mark 7:24–37, November 2nd, 2014

During the week, I had to choose an Old Testament reading to accompany the passage that is part of our sermon series on Mark's Gospel account. The Rector's Warden gave me my instructions: choose one without difficult-to-pronounce names!

Instead, it's the Mark passage that has the names and even a word in Aramaic. If you'd like to turn to our passage, it's on p. 976 of the church Bibles. Mk. ch. 7 beginning at v. 24. The first heading the NIV provides is "The faith of the Syrophoenician Woman". The place of Tyre is mentioned and Syrian Phoenicia, then Sidon and the Decapolis and finally our lesson in Aramaic, *Ephphatha*.

Why does the Bible contain words with which we're unfamiliar? Is it just to provide lesson-readers with a challenge? Any good translation, however 'with it' it might be, needs to come to terms with the fact that the Bible, originally written in Hebrew, Aramaic and Greek, was written a long time ago in a specific cultural and geographic context.

There are names around BC with which we are very familiar and which have significance for us. When I signed up with Shaw I was given a password: Squamish. And if you'd asked me to spell Sechelt, I wouldn't have got it right. East Hastings probably brings to mind particular associations: it certainly does for Miles who found himself wandering there, fortunately not after dark.

This is how it would have been for the Bible's original recipients. They were familiar with the names and they would have meant something to them. We have to do a bit more work.

V. 24, "Jesus left that place and went to the vicinity of Tyre." V. 31, "Then Jesus left the vicinity of Tyre and went through Sidon, down to the Sea of Galilee and into the region of the Decapolis." The inclusion of place names helps ground the narrative in reality. These were actual places with real people: we're not talking of Narnia! But I think Mark gives these details to convey additional meaning. The clue is in the name *Decapolis*. It's a Greek word meaning "ten cities". And this tells us that the area was Greek, Gentile, not Jewish. And the same is the case for Tyre and Sidon, both of which are cities in what is now Lebanon. Back in the day, they were Greek cities.

Dare I mention the 's word' in the context of Holy Trinity? Sabbatical. Don't worry, I'm not about to ask for one; indeed, there was a specific question on this matter as part of the interview process! But Jesus' journey to Tyre, Sidon and the Decapolis may be considered as a sort of Sabbatical. Jesus' reason for going there was probably that he was hoping for a bit of peace and quiet. He wanted to spend some time teaching his disciples. He didn't go there thinking he was going to minister to Gentiles. He'd been ministering to the Jews of the other regions and now he was going away for a rest.

Jesus takes himself to Tyre and "entered a house and did not want anyone to know it." This was probably part of his desire for Sabbatical rest. It may be part of what is known as the Messianic Secret: he didn't want word to spread about him before he had had time to prepare his disciples by teaching them. Something picked up again in v. 36: "Jesus commanded them not to tell anyone." And it may have been because at this time he considered his ministry to be to Jews, not to Gentiles.

But something happened. The Syrophoenician woman appears. Since she was Greek and from Syrian Phoenicia, the assumption is that she was sophisticated and rich. And yet she "fell at [Jesus'] feet" and "begged" him on behalf of her "little daughter who was possessed by an evil spirit". It appears that Jesus' fame had spread, or else the woman was particularly discerning.

In response Jesus says to her, v. 27, "it is not right to take the children's bread and toss it to their dogs." I've heard it said that this isn't as abrasive as it might sound. Jesus is just speaking in parable. He's using picture language that the woman would understand as a pet-lover. Indeed, the Greek word used may be translated as doggies or puppies; think of Margaret's pet pooch

Benny. Furthermore, the Greek construction in v. 29 may be considered as saying, the demon has already left your daughter. Perhaps the miracle had already happened when the woman first spoke to Jesus, and he just wanted to draw her into conversation in order to strengthen her faith in him.

But I'm not so sure. The phrase "the children's bread" makes me think of the children of Israel, the Jews. And it's hard not to think that Jesus is making a comparison between Gentiles and dogs, not a flattering comparison, however loveable the pooches may be.

I've mentioned the possibility of the Syrophoenician woman's discernment regarding who Jesus was and what he could do for her daughter. Perhaps her reply to Jesus, "Yes, Lord, but even the dogs under the table eat the children's crumbs" is a real epiphany moment for him. In Phil. ch. 2, Paul talks of Jesus' "self-emptying"; the Greek word is *kenosis*: the relinquishment of divine attributes by Jesus in becoming human.

I believe that Jesus' ministry and his understanding of it evolved. To the point that in the Great Commission at the end of Matthew's Gospel account, Jesus tells the disciples to "go and make disciples of all nations" [Mt. 28:19]. Perhaps Jesus' encounter with the Syrophoenician woman was a turning-point in his understanding of his mission.

It is remarkable that the first person Mark records as addressing Jesus as Lord is not one of the disciples, but the Syrophoenician woman. The disciples had been unable to understand Jesus' parables without his explaining them. "They had not understood about the [Feeding of the Five Thousand] because their hearts were hardened" [Mk. 6:52]. Yet the woman instantly says, "Yes, Lord." And she recognises that Jesus' grace is such that only a crumb is required in order to be efficacious, akin to faith as small as a mustard seed.

This encounter has entered Anglican liturgy, as part of what's known as the Prayer of Humble Access: "We are not worthy So much as to gather up the crumbs under thy Table. But thou art the same Lord, Whose property is always to have mercy."

Jesus would have had the Syrophoenician woman's reply ringing in his ears when he encountered the Greek man of the Decapolis. We might say that he'd had his ears opened by his encounter with the woman. And then he met a man who was deaf and had an impediment in his speech.

I wonder if you're someone who struggles with hearing, or perhaps you know someone who does. One of the handicaps of being deaf is that people tend to leave you out of the conversation. Here are some things said by deaf people:

'I can't hear. Unless someone makes it clear that I am being talked to, I assume everyone is leaving me out'.

'I can't hear. For most of the time, as far as other people are concerned, I needn't exist.'

'I can't hear. I judge by the way people look, the things they do, the way they touch, not by what they say.'

At this point I'd like to make a distinction, if I may, between a disability and a handicap. A disability is a malfunction of muscle or ear or eye. It is a fact of life and often can't be altered. A handicap is largely a matter of people's attitudes to the disability, whether of the person themselves or of their community, and often this can be altered.

The man in the story has a triple handicap. He is a Gentile, so a social and religious outcast; he is deaf, so people talk round him, and because he can't hear, he hasn't been able to listen to people speaking, so his own speech has been impeded.

Notice how Jesus approaches him. First he takes him aside, making it clear he wants to communicate with him directly and not through others. Then he uses signs: putting his fingers in the man's ears and touching his tongue with spittle from his own tongue. It may sound somewhat crude, but it is a very direct and earthy way of communicating with the man and letting him know what Jesus is going to do. This man who has been excluded and closed-off from the community for too long — as it were excommunicated — is now going to be included again.

Only then does Jesus speak, and just one word. The actual Aramaic word has been recorded for us, *Eph-pha-tha*, an absolute gift for lip-reading. In English its meaning is 'be opened'. The life of this closed-off man is now reopened. At this, "People were overwhelmed with amazement", v. 37, " 'He has done everything well' they said", reminiscent of creation, when God made all things good.

The deaf man, we are told, has a speech impediment: he "could hardly speak". Here Mark uses a very unusual Greek word, *mogilalos*, meaning speaking with difficulty or stammering. In the whole Greek Bible there is only one other occurrence of this word, in Is. ch. 35, (our Old Testament reading). I believe that Mark chose the word intentionally, to link what was occurring with Isaiah's prophecy. When the day of the Lord comes, says Isaiah, this is how it will be, v. 5: "Then will the eyes of the blind be opened, and the ears of the deaf unstopped; then will the lame leap like a deer, and the mute [the *mogilalos*] tongue shout for joy."

On Thursday, I was discussing with Margaret, a VST student, her MA on eschatological spirituality, how the vision of how things will be at the end times, after Jesus' return, can be realised in the here and now. It was passages such as Is. 35 that inspired the American painter Edward Hicks, famous for his depictions of the Peaceable Kingdom.

Our Lord's message to the disciples and therefore to us is: the day of the Lord is at hand; in Jesus God has come to save his people; his people are not just the Jews, but the Gentile world as well. In God's kingdom the excluded will be included, the last will be first, and handicaps will fall away.

I made a distinction between disability and handicap. In doing so, I'm not saying that Jesus didn't effect a very real healing, removing a disability. And such things do also occur today, either through medical science or through the healing ministry of the Church. But many people aren't healed in that way. Their disability remains. What of them? This is where our attitude comes into play, in determining to what extent a disability is to be a handicap.

When in England, I used to visit the resort of Scarborough. Part of the attraction is the wonderful Spa Orchestra, the last remaining professional seaside orchestra in the UK. At one of their concerts the singer Sir Willard White sang. In the course of the evening he made an appeal on behalf of the North Yorkshire Music Therapy Centre, a charity with which he's associated. Their stated aim is to "help vulnerable people to express themselves and to communicate with others." It struck me, when listening to what the charity was endeavouring to do, that they set a good example of reaching out to others so that disability needn't be an unnecessary handicap.

Our job, as Christians, followers of Jesus, is to communicate with all those who may have been excommunicated by others or, more often these days, have excommunicated themselves. We are to draw people to God, to share with them the good news of the Gospel. Then the hungry of body or soul will receive more than the scraps which fall from the table, those who now feel their lives are bound and limited will be released, and the formerly tongue-tied will sing for joy!

Well, that's the challenge. If you perhaps feel intimidated by it, then take heart. Remember that Jesus himself may have learnt as he went along, through his encounter with the woman and with others. Just be open to the encounters with which God will strew your way and be open to what God can teach you through them.

Amen.

Mark 8:1–21, November 9th, 2014

There's something I did from day one here at Holy Trinity. Indeed, I think I mentioned it at interview and so raised it to pretty much a condition of coming here. I did so because it's something I'd instituted during my time in the parishes where I was before and I found it made a big difference. It certainly helped me a lot as a preacher. Has that got you wondering?

What I'm referring to is sequential preaching through books of the Bible. This isn't the only way to preach of course. And we'll be taking a break during Advent and Christmas as we look at themes to do with those seasons.

Let me try and illustrate why I find sequential reading and preaching of the Bible helpful, with reference to our passage from Mk. ch. 8, which you'll find on p. 976 of the church Bibles. The NIV heads the first section, The Feeding of the Four Thousand. I hope that makes you think of the passage we looked at five weeks ago, from Mk. ch. 6: Jesus Feeds the Five Thousand.

Let's face it, the accounts of the feeding of the four and the five thousands are remarkably similar. So much so that some have suggested that they may be two accounts of the same incident. If you look hard enough, you'll find commentators who say just about anything about any Bible passage, much of which is wrong. That the suggestion that the two passages are in fact one is an example of such muddle-headedness is, to my mind, clearly demonstrated by the fact that in v. 19 Jesus refers to the five thousand as a separate incident.

So we're left with the question 'Why?' Why has Mark, along with Matthew, provided accounts of both incidents? An answer, a good one, is that they both took place and each is a significant event. But Mark is economical in his gospel account. It's the shortest: just 16 chapters and there's plenty that he doesn't include as part of his account of three years of ministry. This should lead us to be particularly interested in why Mark includes something. And the feeding of the four thousand isn't in Luke.

Our sequential reading has more to offer. What were we looking at last week in the passage immediately before? Perhaps you'll recall that we were in Gentile, non-Jewish territory: Tyre, Sidon, the Decapolis. And Jesus appears to have had his eyes opened. He finds himself ministering, perhaps unexpectedly, to a Syrophoenician woman and a deaf and mute man, also, presumably, Gentile, on the basis of the locale.

Mk. 8 begins, "During those days", indicating continuity with what was before; Jesus was still in the Decapolis, Gentile territory. In Matthew's account of the feeding of the four thousand he records that "these people", upon whom Jesus had compassion, were led to "praise the God of Israel" [Mt. 15:31]. If they were Jewish, of Israel, it would be more natural just to say 'they praised God.'

This all points to the fact that whereas the five thousand had been Jewish, the four thousand were Gentile. The feeding of the four thousand continues the inclusivity of Gentiles, non-Jews, established previously through Jesus' ministry to the Syrophoenician woman and the Gentile deaf and mute man. Jesus provides for all. Jesus is saviour of all. That is what Mark wants us to hear through his inclusion of the four thousand in addition to the five thousand, coming immediately after what had occurred in ch. 7.

The repeat of the miracle also seems necessary because of the disciples' apparent failure to learn from what occurred before. V. 4, "His disciples answered, 'But where in this remote place can anyone get enough bread to feed them?' " Duh: answers on a postcard please!

And their continual failure to grasp what was going on is recorded in merciless detail. " 'Be careful,' Jesus warned them" in v. 15. I think if Jesus told me to "be careful" I'd try to be particularly careful. But when Jesus follows with "Watch out for the yeast of the Pharisees and that of Herod", how do the disciples respond?

V. 16, "They discussed this with one another and said 'It is because we have no bread.' "

I'm sorry, but if anyone, let alone Jesus, were to say to you "Watch out for the yeast of the Pharisees and that of Herod", would the most natural conclusion be that "It is because we have no bread"? I think I'd deduce that something else was going on, other than failure to make adequate sandwich provision for a boat trip! Jesus apparently, is also of this opinion. V. 17: "Aware of their discussion, Jesus asked them: 'Why are you talking about having no bread? Do you still not see or understand? Are your hearts hardened? Do you have eyes but fail to see, and ears but fail to hear? And don't you remember?' "

I described the account of the disciples' failure to understand as being merciless. And you might be particularly feeling that, given that serve from Jesus. But remember who's giving us this account — Mark. This is the same Mark who had deserted Paul during his first missionary journey [Acts 13:13]. Paul subsequently refused to take Mark with him on his second missionary journey [Acts 15:38]. But by the end of his life, Mark was to fully regain Paul's favour [II Tim. 4:11].

And Mark's gospel account of what occurred came from Peter who had been directly involved. They're being brutally honest about their own limitations. Mark and Peter are saying to us, look, we made mistakes and you will too. But that's not the end of things. And you can learn through our mistakes, our failure to understand at the time.

Jesus holds out more hope for them than perhaps the NIV's translation of vv. 17 and 21 allows. I'd suggest that "Do you still not understand?" is more appropriately translated as "Do you not yet understand?" By which Jesus indicates that their understanding will come. So take heart if you find things difficult to understand!

Having established that Jesus' reference to yeast is nothing to do with the disciples having forgotten to bring enough bread, what is it about? Every time yeast is referred to in the New Testament, with the exception of once in Matthew, it is used as a symbol of evil or corruption: so, what Jesus is saying is, "Watch out for the corruption of the Pharisees and that of Herod."

The Pharisees and Herodians have already been seen together as an unholy alliance in opposition to Jesus, back in ch. 3: "Then the Pharisees ... began to plot with the Herodians how they might kill Jesus." Their desire to kill Jesus was the outworking of their corruption.

In the case of the Pharisees, the root of their corruption was their blinkered theological mindset. Jesus just couldn't be made to fit in with where they were coming from theologically. And this was particularly obvious because Jesus was there in person; they were able to interact with him directly. Jesus spoke plainly to the Pharisees but at the same time he "sighed deeply", v. 12, knowing what was in their hearts; Jesus presents himself to people but he doesn't force himself upon them.

In our age, there are people like this, who dismiss Jesus because they reject what he stands for. I find it remarkable that this rejection is often without even making an attempt to discern whether Christianity is true or not. They've already got a mindset that has determined that it's irrelevant. For myself, I knew that Christianity was of such potential importance, that I decided to find out for myself whether or not it is true. And my answer was, yes it is.

In addition to those who dismiss Jesus, there are others who claim to follow him, yet pick and choose or distort his teaching. They fit Jesus into their mindset, taking the bits they like and rejecting the rest. Ultimate religious consumerism.

I used to do orienteering, running around the countryside with a compass, trying to follow a route on the map. One time (actually more than one time!) I got hopelessly lost. I then tried to convince myself that I knew where I was on the map by linking landscape features with lines on the map that clearly didn't fit. That's what some try to do with Jesus: make him fit in with their view of things.

King Herod's corruption was one of morality. He had persuaded his brother's wife to leave her husband and marry him instead. And then he had John the Baptist put to death, in spite of knowing him to be "a righteous and holy man" [Mk. 6:20]. We're told that Herod "liked to listen to [John]." He liked to listen to his sermons. But he failed to act upon them.

I'm reminded of Paul preaching to the learned men of Athens on the Areopagus in Acts 17:32: "When they heard about the resurrection of the dead, some of them sneered, but others said, 'We want to hear you again on this subject' ". I'm not sure what's worse, the sneering or viewing preaching as a mere exercise in intellectual stimulation.

My answer to all this is again, sequential Bible reading. This is also why I like the Scripture Union's Bible reading notes, because they work progressively through Bible books. Doing this means we're more likely to encounter Jesus as he truly is, on his own terms; Rather than taking a selective approach which ends up seeing him on our terms and therefore effectively not at all.

V. 19, Jesus asks the disciples how many baskets of bread were left over after feeding the five thousand: the answer was twelve. And for the four thousand there were seven baskets of leftovers. Jesus said to them, "Do you not yet understand?"

The numbers of baskets are irrelevant apart from this one fact, there's a lot left over! We read at v. 8, "The people ate and were satisfied." And even when they've done so, there are plenty of leftovers.

Friends, God's provision is not just sufficient, it's overflowing, there's an abundance. That's the type of God we encounter when we truly get to know Jesus. One who provides for our deepest needs. Not the superficial things we might think we need. But our spiritual hunger. Our need for spiritual feeding. His grace is abundant.

The leftovers and the fact that Jesus repeats the miracle underlines the fact that his grace is more than sufficient for all the people of the whole world: Jew or Gentile. His grace can deal with all sin, past, present and future. To receive his grace and mercy all that is required is to encounter and follow the real Jesus, to be in relationship with him as your personal Lord and Saviour.

Amen.

Mark 8:22–30, November 16th, 2014

There are 16 chapters in Mark's Gospel account. So, where does the midway point come? You can do the math: ch. 8, which is our reading for today. May I encourage you to turn to it; it's on p. 977 in the church Bibles, Mk. ch. 8, vv. 22–30.

Mark's is the earliest Gospel account. It's sometimes regarded as a bit 'rough and ready'. It's the shortest; somewhat pithy and punchy; the Greek in which it's written isn't the most sophisticated. But that doesn't mean that it's without style and structure. Mark has a message he wants to get across and he's planned out how to do it.

This passage, at the heart of his work, is a crucial turning-point that he's been working up to. Something in it is very important for what he wants to say. It's in the section the NIV has headed Peter's confession of Christ. V. 27: Jesus asked his disciples, "Who do people say I am?"

Mark has already provided variants on this. Think back to Jesus' calming of the storm. Afterward, at the end of ch. 4, the disciples asked each other, "Who is this? Even the wind and the waves obey him!" At ch. 1, v. 27, we read: "The people were all so amazed that they asked each other, 'What is this? A new teaching — and with authority! He [Jesus] gives orders to evil spirits and they obey him.' "

The evil spirits knew who Jesus is. Ch. 1, v. 24: "A man ... who was possessed by an evil spirit cried out 'What do you want with us, Jesus of Nazareth? ... I know who you are, the Holy One of God!' " Chapter five, v. 7: a man with an evil spirit "shouted at the top of his voice, 'What do you want with me, Jesus, Son of the Most High God?' "

Mark wanted us, his readers, to know the answer right from the start. At Jesus' baptism in ch. 1, "a voice came from heaven: 'You are my Son, whom I love; with you I am well pleased.' " In Mark's account, the voice speaks directly to Jesus. But Mark wants us to be in on the information. It's as if we're watching a drama unfold, knowing something that the characters struggle to grasp. Perhaps we find ourselves egging them on: "Don't you get it yet?"

We've got some way to go in our preaching series before we reach ch. 15. But perhaps you already know v. 39. I'm afraid that I can't read it without thinking of John Wayne, who spoke the verse in the film *The Greatest Story Ever Told*: "When the centurion, who stood there in front of Jesus, heard his cry and saw how he died, he said, 'truly this man was the Son of God.' " Mark wants to leave us in no doubt about this fact.

V. 27 of our passage in ch. 8: Jesus asked his disciples, "Who do people say I am?" Don't you just love it when someone comes out with, "People are saying"? It's a way of saying, this is what I think. So what are people saying? V. 28, "Some say John the Baptist; others say Elijah; and still others, one of the prophets."

We might be tempted to settle for this. A lesser Jesus but in good company. I think it's in the film *Paradise Road* that the Japanese commandant of the internment camp declares, "Japanese Empire number one, British Empire number ten." I think that I and the friend with whom I'd watched the movie came away thinking he'd been fairly decent to give us number ten slot! Actually, we were meant to understand that the scale ran only from one to ten.

People had got it wrong about Jesus. Yes, good company: John the Baptist, Elijah, the prophets. But if we were to settle for this, we'd be underselling Jesus. People do so. They settle for a lesser Jesus. But this doesn't make sense. It doesn't fit in with what we've been shown about Jesus, what he's done. And it doesn't fit in with what Jesus says about himself.

C.S. Lewis wrote in his book *Mere Christianity*: "I am trying here to prevent anyone saying the really foolish thing that people often say about [Jesus]: I'm ready to accept Jesus as a great moral teacher, but I don't accept his claim to be God. That is the one thing we must not say. A man who was merely a man and said the sort of things Jesus said would not be a great moral teacher.

He would either be a lunatic — on the level with the man who says he is a poached egg — or else he would be the Devil of Hell. You must make your choice. Either this man was, and is, the Son of God, or else a madman or something worse."

Jesus now turns the spotlight directly on the disciples. V. 29: " 'But what about you?' he asked, 'Who do you say I am?' " It's the same question that Jesus directs at us. And we must answer it for ourselves, not on the basis of the opinions of others. "Who do you say I am?" Peter gives his answer. Wonderful, impetuous Peter who, I'm afraid, so often gets it wrong, this time gets it right: "Peter answered, 'You are the Christ.' "

What does it mean to say that Jesus is the Christ? It's the same word as Messiah, one is Greek the other Hebrew. The Messiah or Christ was the one whom the Jews were waiting for. He was God's anointed one. It's akin to Holy One of God, Son of the Most High God: the evil spirits got it right.

The Messiah was to be the go-between between God and his people: the mediator. He would rule for ever and those who accepted his reign would be brought into God's family for ever. To believe in the Messiah is to believe that God saves his people, he forgives their sins, God calls his people to himself through the Messiah.

That's why confessing Jesus as the Christ is at the heart of being a Christian, as the name suggests. To be a Christian is to say, 'I believe that Jesus is the Christ'. If you don't believe that, then it doesn't make much sense being a Christian. It would make more sense in that case to follow the Jewish religion.

Most Jews are still waiting for the coming of the Messiah on the basis that Jesus wasn't the Christ. Unfortunately, that also means that you're stuck under the Old Testament law approach to religion, being aware of your failure to keep God's law but without the love and forgiveness that Jesus is able to offer us as the Christ.

Jesus being the Christ is such good news, we might find ourselves wondering why more people don't embrace that belief, indeed, why everyone doesn't. Remember what Jesus said in last week's reading. V. 17: "Do you not yet see or understand? Are your hearts hardened?" To have a hard heart is to be unable to accept a spiritual truth. It's like ground that is baked so hard that water can't penetrate. And people can be spiritually blind.

That's why Mark places the healing of the blind man at Bethsaida immediately before Peter's confession of Christ. This was an actual physical healing: I don't want to take away from that. But Mark's telling of this miracle gives us more. People who are spiritually blind can have their eyes opened by God. The things that prevent them from seeing the truth about Jesus are what he referred to in v. 15 as "the yeast of the Pharisees and that of Herod." Yeast is the Bible's way of referring to corruption, the sin that separates us from God. Jesus warns us to "be careful" of this. When faced with the Pharisees, Jesus "sighed deeply". He does so, because he's not going to force himself on anyone; they have to be willing to accept him.

The two-stage healing of the blind man is an important part of this. V. 23, "Jesus asked [the man], 'Do you see anything?' He looked up and said, 'I see people; they look like trees walking around.'" The man's healing was gradual. It took more than one go. And that's what it can be like with people's coming to faith in Jesus. It may not happen immediately, but over time.

V. 25: "Once more Jesus put his hands on the man's eyes. Then his eyes were opened, his sight was restored, and he saw everything clearly." Just as the man came to see clearly, people who have a distorted picture of Jesus can have their eyes opened and see him clearly for who he is: "You are the Christ".

God plays a part in this, just as Jesus did in healing the blind man. But people's hearts also need to be softened, to be receptive. A hard heart is unable to accept Jesus for who he is: the Christ. To soften one's heart is to be careful, to watch out for the yeast, the corruption, of the Pharisees and that of Herod: the sin that separates us from God.

This is something of which we need to be aware. The Christian path is not always an easy one to travel. There are likely to be wobbles, even what the Bible refers to as "backsliding". Peter found this out. Immediately after getting it right and confessing Jesus as the Christ, Peter was to get it terribly wrong, earning the rebuke from Jesus, "Get behind me, Satan", v. 33. He was later to deny even knowing Jesus: "I don't know this man you're talking about", ch. 14, v. 71.

The way we live our lives as Christians is important for us in our relation with God. We need to be aware of this for the sake of ourselves. But also for the sake of others, to whom we seek to witness what it means to say of Jesus, "You are the Christ". We are to do as Peter did, confessing with our mouth that Jesus is the Christ: he is our Lord and Saviour. And we help others to hear this by the way that we live our lives as those who see Jesus clearly for who he is. In this way we can help with softening the hearts of others. So that they too, perhaps after a period of time, may come to see Jesus clearly for who he is and may join Peter's confession: "You are the Christ".

Amen.

Mark 8:31–9:1, February 22nd, 2015

Please turn to our passage, Mk. ch. 8 beginning at v. 31, which you'll find on p. 977 in the church Bibles. We left off from our studies in Mark's Gospel account in mid-November. Since then we've had Advent, Christmas, Epiphany and our studies in the Book of Psalms.

Let me refresh your memory regarding where we got to. The first point is an easy one: ch. 8 is the midway point in the account. Second, this juncture is a crucial turning-point in the narrative. Which leads me to my third point: in v. 29 Peter is recorded as saying of Jesus, "You are the Christ." That segment in the NIV is headed 'Peter's Confession of Christ.'

We can see this as a high point. It's taken eight chapters to get there, but Peter's said it: "You are the Christ." Then our passage begins, v. 31, "[Jesus] then began to teach the [disciples]"; and, v. 32, "He spoke plainly." Up until now, Jesus has tended to speak somewhat obliquely, often by means of parables. Now he's speaking plainly, notwithstanding the fact that he's just told the disciples "not to tell anyone about him", presumably, not to tell others at this point that he's the Christ or Messiah.

In 1982 F.R. David sang 'Words don't come easy'; ah, music of my lifetime! Trouble is, sometimes they come all too easily and people don't necessarily mean what they say. Peter has a bit of a pedigree for that, blurting things out, seemingly unthinkingly. When he said, "You are the Christ", did he mean it?

Let's be generous and give him the benefit of the doubt. Next question, did he know what he was saying? Possibly not. There was a current perception of what the Christ or Messiah (it's the same word) meant. Most often it was thought of in terms of someone God was to provide as a great military leader for the Jews and, in that context, it would have meant someone who was going to get rid of the Romans.

Jesus would have known this and hence he immediately begins

"to teach the disciples ... plainly"; some straight talking about what kind of Christ he was, knowing that this didn't fit in with expectations. This is what he said: "The Son of Man [his way of referring to himself] must suffer many things and be rejected by the elders, Chief Priests and Teachers of the Law, and that he must be killed and after three days rise again."

I read an obituary for Adrien Dubois who died on December 12th. He sounded like a nasty piece of work, described as "a scion of Montreal's brotherhood of crime." Not the sort of person you'd want to cross with or meet on a dark night.

One of the remarkable things Jesus says is that he's going to be rejected and killed by the Jewish religious establishment. This is not what you expect to hear about the Messiah. Killed by thugs, perhaps, but not by those who were 'respectable' and who you'd think would welcome him.

I suspect that Peter didn't really hear the bit about Jesus rising again after three days. Perhaps that sounded like fanciful talk. He appears incensed at the prospect of Jesus' being rejected and then killed. And so Peter takes Jesus aside and begins to rebuke him.

I have a vision of Peter physically manhandling Jesus. And that word rebuke is strong stuff. In ch. 9, v. 25, we're told of Jesus rebuking an evil spirit; that was the sort of word it was. It's a remarkable scene, Peter basically telling Jesus that he doesn't know what he's talking about.

Sermon illustrations must come with caveats. For example, it's impossible to illustrate the Trinity without falling into heresy of one sort or another. The territory I'm about to enter is fraught with danger, because it may seem to compare Jesus with me! But stick with me, let's run it up the flagpole and see if it flaps in the wind!

Two incidents from my curacy in Chester-le-Street in the North East of England. I was sitting in the Parish Centre, drinking a cup of coffee, wearing my clerical collar. "Was I on my day off?" I was asked. And again, I encountered a startled parishioner in the supermarket and was asked, "What are you doing here?"

I read into this that people have a strange view of clergy as people somehow detached from the real world. They're the sort of people who would put on a clerical collar and go to the Parish Centre on their day off because, what else would they do? And we're so other-worldly that it's difficult to imagine us shopping for groceries! From this comes the idea that we don't understand the ways of the world.

I think Peter thought Jesus needed saving from himself. As far as Peter was concerned, Jesus was talking nonsense and needed to be brought back on track. Jesus, typical clergyman, didn't really understand the world and what was required.

Peter thought he was talking sense and in his terms, he was. But for his efforts, he's in turn the recipient of a stinging rebuke from Jesus. Bear in mind that Mark probably heard about what occurred directly from Peter: talk about having to eat humble pie!

V. 33: "Jesus turned and looked at his disciples", the rebuke was to be witnessed by them, "Get behind me, Satan! ... You do not have in mind the things of God, but the things of men." Ouch. Peter might have had a comeback if it had just been about things of God versus things of men. Perhaps he might have argued that the two weren't incompatible. But Jesus' identification of him with Satan put a stop to that.

The cross is central to Christianity; and it must be central in our understanding of Jesus. Satan can just about cope with Jesus' being identified as the Christ. James writes in his Epistle, ch. 2, v. 19, "You say you have faith, for you believe that there is one God. Good for you! Even the demons believe this, and they tremble in terror" (NLT). Then James continues: "You foolish man, do you want evidence that faith without deeds is useless?" He illustrates his point with Abraham. Abraham's faith was demonstrated by his willingness to sacrifice his son Isaac, not that in the end he was required to do so.

Words can come easily. They can represent what Dietrich Bonhoeffer referred to as 'cheap grace'. And Bonhoeffer knew what he was talking about because he was to pay with his life for his Christian faith.

We may say that Jesus is the Christ. But do we mean what we say? And do we understand what it means? Christianity is under pressure, from both outside and inside the Church. The temptation is to follow and present another Jesus; one who fits in with what we want from him, just what Peter was trying to achieve.

But the only real Jesus is the one who embraced the cross. The cross wasn't a tragic accident. Note the emphatic "must": "the Son of Man must suffer ... and be rejected ... [and] he must be killed." This was so because it was God's will that Jesus was following.

This doesn't make sense in worldly terms. But it's only through the cross that Satan was defeated. That's why Satan, through Peter, seeks to divert Jesus from it. "Get behind me, Satan!"

Bonhoeffer wrote a book called *The Cost of Discipleship*; that's what Jesus talks about in vv. 34–38: the cost of discipleship. Do you consider yourself a disciple of Jesus? 'Disciple' is used far more frequently in the New Testament than the word Christian. Sometimes it refers to the Twelve. But it came to mean all who are Christian. To be Christian is to be one of Jesus' disciples, one of his followers. In the next section, Jesus is addressing "the crowd"; he tells them, this is what it means for anyone to be one of his followers; it's not meant for just the elite few.

Jesus says, v. 34, "If anyone would come after me, he must deny himself and take up his cross and follow me." We may think of being a Christian in terms of denying ourselves something or other. But what Jesus says is more radical. It's not deny ourselves *something*; it's deny *ourselves*. What does this mean?

The clue is in "take up his cross." We may talk glibly about having a cross to bear, meaning some minor burden. But taking up the cross involves fully identifying ourselves with Jesus. It means putting Christ crucified at the centre of our lives. Living lives that are not 'me'-centred, but Christ-centred. Joining with Jesus in the Garden of Gethsemane, saying to God the Father, "Not my will, but yours be done", Lk. 22:42.

I've mentioned previously the paradoxes intrinsic to Christianity. Here's one of them, v. 35: "Whoever wants to save his life will lose it, but whoever loses his life for me and for the gospel will save it." We may baulk at the idea of handing over our lives. But remember to whom it is that we're called to do this: God. Our lives are his anyway: he made us. Bending our wills to his is merely things as they are, or rather, as they should be.

V. 36, "What good is it for a man to gain the whole world, yet forfeit his soul?" What a wonderful and key verse. The *Globe and Mail* has been edging around this theme of late, doing so on its own terms of course. There was an invitation for readers to give advice to their younger selves. The gist was that there's more to life than the materialistic goals a twenty-something would naturally set.

On January 1st there was, "Top 15 tips for a healthier, happier 2015", which included: "Talk to your teen like an adult"; "Connect with someone"; "Break bread together" (that's an interesting one); "Take charge of technology". The overall thrust might be summed up as, "No-one at the end of his life says, 'I wish I'd spent more time at the office.'"

The problem with *The Globe*'s approach is that while putting materialism in its place, it doesn't have anything with ultimate meaning to replace it with. The nearest Zo Michele of Halifax got, when writing to her younger self, was: "You're going to learn many things, outside of the classroom: A Buddhist meditation group will teach you to value faith as well as knowledge. You'll learn to become a person who does not need to strive to be anything in order to find fulfilment, your most important lesson."

That seems to be all *The Globe* can offer. Perhaps yoga, or meditation, or New Age spirituality. What Jesus is offering, if we follow his way, is the prospect of eternal life with him. Put it this way and anything the world can give seems paltry by comparison.

When Jesus talks about "this adulterous ... generation" he isn't referring to sexual sin. Adultery here means seeking after other gods, other things, other goals, other than him. You see, it's got to be all or nothing. You can't have a bit of man's way, a bit of my way, and a bit of God's way; they just aren't compatible, contrary to what Peter might have thought.

I've posted on the church's Facebook page a link to what I hope is a helpful summary of the gospel: Two Ways to Live. In summary, this is what it says:

1. God is the loving ruler of the world. He made the world. He made us rulers of the world under him. But is that the way it is now?

2. We all reject the ruler, God, by trying to run life our own way without him. But we fail to rule ourselves or society or the world. What will God do about this rebellion?

3. God won't let us rebel forever. God's punishment for rebellion is death and judgement. God's justice sounds hard. But ...

4. Because of his love, God sent his son into the world: the man Jesus Christ. Jesus always lived under God's rule. Yet in dying in our place he took our punishment and brought forgiveness. But that's not all ...

5. God raised Jesus to life again as ruler of the world. Jesus has conquered death, now gives life, and will return to judge. Well, where does that leave us?

6. The two ways to live:

    a. Our way: reject the ruler, God; try to run life our way. Result: condemned by God; facing death and judgement.

    b. God's new way: submit to Jesus as our ruler; rely on Jesus' death and resurrection. Result: forgiven by God; given eternal life.

That's the choice with which each one of us is faced: do we choose to live our way or God's way? Although we need to make this choice for ourselves as individuals, having done so, we are not on our own. God is not only our Creator; Jesus is our companion on the way; and the Holy Spirit guides us and comforts us.

The fellowship of the Church is there to help us, bearing one another's burdens. And I hope that courses such as ReFrame help us with the question of faithful discipleship in our everyday lives.

We can take comfort from these words of Jesus:

Mt. 11:28-30, "Come to me, all you who are weary and burdened, and I will give you rest. Take my yoke upon you and learn from me, for I am gentle and humble in heart, and you will find rest for your souls. For my yoke is easy and my burden is light."

And these of Paul, I Cor. 10:13: "God is faithful; he will not let you be tempted beyond what you can bear. But when you are tempted, he will also provide a way out so that you can endure it." And II Cor. 12:9: "[Jesus] said to me, 'My grace is sufficient for you.'"

Amen.

Mark 9:2–13, March 1st, 2015

We believe in a God who cares for us and wants to be intimately involved with us. That was why he created us: "God saw all that he had made and it was very good", Gen. 1:31. In Gen. 3:8 we read of God "walking in the garden [of Eden]." He cared for the Israelites, so he provided a leader for them, Moses. As the Israelites journeyed through the wilderness, "By day the Lord went ahead of them in a pillar of cloud to guide them on their way", Ex. 13:21.

God met with Moses on Mount Sinai and gave him the Law, Ex. 24:15: "When Moses went up on the mountain, the cloud covered it, and the glory of the Lord settled on Mount Sinai". Later in Old Testament history, God provided prophets for Israel, the greatest of whom was Elijah. God cares for his creation and for its pinnacle, mankind. He wants to know his people and to be known by them. That is why he reveals himself and his will to us. He's no absentee landlord; he gets down and gets involved.

In the New Testament, the Epistle to the Hebrews begins: "In the past God spoke to our forefathers through the prophets at many times and in various ways, but in these last days he has spoken to us by his Son ... The Son is the radiance of God's glory and the exact representation of his being." With Jesus, God has cranked up his involvement to the ultimate level; he comes in the person of his Son. Jesus, being both God and man, facilitates a relationship between God and his creation in a way that had not been possible since the Fall, the sin of Adam and Eve in the Garden of Eden: something that has tainted creation ever since.

In our studies in Mark's gospel account we've reached ch. 9. I invite you to turn to it, it's on p. 978 in the church Bibles. You'll see it's headed The Transfiguration. That's our topic. You may know a lot about the Transfiguration already or you may just have heard about it as a term, in art for example. Whatever is the case, I hope you'll know a little more about it and its relevance by the end!

In chapters one to eight the disciples, and we as readers, have been getting to know more about Jesus. The things they've experienced have led to them to ponder the question: "Who is this?" ch. 4, v. 41. This was in response to Jesus' calming a storm. In addition, there have been two incidents of thousands of people being miraculously fed, healings and the bringing back to life of a dead girl. Plenty of examples of Jesus' concern for people and his involvement with and authority over both physical creation and the spiritual domain.

This led, in ch. 8, to Peter's confession of Jesus as the Christ or Messiah. And Jesus telling the disciples what sort of Christ he was and what following him meant in terms of suffering and death, as well as resurrection and eternal life.

Maybe after this the disciples were hoping for some reassurance and comfort. And maybe they got more than they were bargaining for! Jesus takes three of them, Peter, James and John, up a high mountain. We're not told which mountain it was, but there's speculation it may have been Mount Hermon. Then we're told, quite abruptly, "He was transfigured before them." What does that mean? What was going on?

The Greek word Mark uses is *metemorphōthē* and it's used in the Bible only in this context. It is, however, from its cognate *metamorphōsis* that we get the word "metamorphosis", used for example of the change in form that some insects undergo, such as from a caterpillar to a butterfly. Jesus' appearance changed: "His clothes became dazzling white, whiter than anyone in the world could bleach them." Then two long-dead figures from the Old Testament appeared and conversed with Jesus: Moses, who had received God's Law, and Elijah, the prophet. Next, a cloud appears and envelops them.

What are we to make of this and what did the disciples make of it? I think the clues are in the fact that it happened on a high mountain, that Jesus' clothes were dazzling, and the presence of the cloud. All of these would have taken the disciples back to the account of Moses' encounter with God on Mount Sinai. They were having an experience akin to what Moses had. They were encountering God in the person of Jesus. To confirm this, there's the voice from the cloud, "This is my Son, whom I love. Listen to him!", echoing the voice from heaven at Jesus' baptism: "You are my Son, whom I love; with you I am well pleased", Mk. 1:11.

In the ReFrame course we've been thinking about the post-resurrection appearance of Jesus to two of the disciples on the road to Emmaus. Lk. ch. 24, v. 25: "[Jesus] said to them, 'How foolish you are, and how slow of heart to believe all that the prophets have spoken. Did not the Christ have to suffer these things and then enter into glory?' And beginning with Moses and all the prophets, he explained to them what was said in all the Scriptures concerning himself." Jesus refers to the Old Testament and says, I am the one to whom Moses and Elijah were pointing, the one they looked forward to.

The appearance of Moses and Elijah at the Transfiguration is physical confirmation of that, right before the eyes of Peter, James and John. We can take comfort from the fact that Moses was there; it marks something of a rehabilitation for him. Moses had not been allowed to enter the Promised Land because he did not trust God enough, and instead was buried outside its border. But now he finds his place alongside Jesus, experiencing God's glory.

Some prefer to concentrate on the New Testament, perhaps to the extent of ignoring the Old Testament. Marcion, in the second century, went so far as saying there were two gods: the Old Testament god of vengeance and the New Testament god of love. Perhaps we've heard echoes of that in our day. But this is not true. There is one God who is to be found in both parts of the Bible. It's true that we look at the Old Testament in the light of Jesus. But equally, we cannot fully know Jesus unless we see him in the light of what the Old Testament says about him.

I've been reading a book entitled *Vancouver: Representing the Postmodern City*. It's a little dated, being published in 1994. But what it says still rings true and the subsequent digital explosion has only added grist to its thesis. Postmodernism is a term that seeks to capture the spirit of our age. It's seen in contrast to Modernism, the long period of Western thought dating back to the 17th century Enlightenment. What's the difference?

The Enlightenment and Modernism are related to the advent of the scientific age, logical thought, and a linear view of things: cause and effect, a progression of events and ideas. This can fit in well with Christianity, which shares some of these characteristics. Indeed, the impetus for the Enlightenment was provided by the 16th century Protestant Reformation.

But there's also been a strand within Modernism that's been dismissive of Christianity: the hard-edged scientific approach that has time only for that which can be seen and touched and measured. In some ways, Richard Dawkins and the 'New Atheists' can be seen as the last gasp of Modernism.

Postmodernism is much more of a mixed bag. It's been described as spatial rather than linear. In other words, going off in all directions at once, grabbing at whatever it can and making use of it. This actually means that it can allow space for the spiritual. The problem is, it's a sort of boundless spirituality, not interested in tradition or making sense of how things relate, they just are.

Christianity, as I've indicated, fits more naturally with Modernist thought. It's a linear religion, one that makes sense of things in terms of a beginning, a middle and an end, with Jesus as the link throughout. But Christianity critiques Modernism by saying that there's more than just the physical and scientific. And Christianity effectively combines the physical with the spiritual.

I started by listing the evidence of God's involvement with and care for his creation and his people. This found ultimate expression in the coming of Jesus, the Incarnation. We've seen in Mark chs. 1–8 Jesus' concern for both the spiritual and physical in his ministry.

At the Transfiguration, Jesus is there, in person, along with Moses and Elijah, also in person: they were no mere chimeras. But the change in Jesus' appearance, his dazzling quality, speaks of the spiritual: it's a revelation of God's glory, embodied in him.

Dear Peter comes in for some criticism. He can suffer from foot-in-mouth disease. But before we're too hard on him, remember we know about incidents such as this because he was the one who told Mark about them. He's saying, learn from my mistakes. V. 5: "Peter said to Jesus, 'Rabbi, it is good for us to be here. Let us put up three shelters — one for you, one for Moses and one for Elijah.' (He did not know what to say, they were so frightened.)"

Peter has previously earned a rebuke from Jesus for trying to dissuade him from his path of suffering and death. I wonder if Peter sought to capture and sustain the glorious occasion of the Transfiguration. Here was good news, much more to his liking, a mountaintop experience.

I wonder too if we can be a bit like that. We have a glorious experience of God and we wish for it to be sustained. If only it could always be like this. I recall a Charlie Brown cartoon where Lucy says, some people have ups and downs, I want to have just ups and ups and ups; in response to which Charlie Brown just groans.

The glory of God can be experienced, but it can't be captured and contained. It can be expressed through the physical but it isn't limited to it. Remember the words of the resurrected Jesus to Mary Magdalene, "Do not hold on to me, for I have not yet returned to my Father", Jn. 20:17.

The Transfiguration is a demonstration of God's ongoing interaction with the physical world and the way he reveals himself through it. It reminds us that Christianity isn't a nebulous faith but one that connects back to physical, historical events. The physicality of our faith was shown in the bodily resurrection of Jesus on that first Easter Day. It is the precursor of our own bodily resurrection, after which we will experience the fullness of God's glory.

Until that time, we can have glimpses of what is to come. For example, in our worship together and particularly in Holy Communion, which, as a sacrament, makes use of physical elements. For those with eyes of faith, the bread and wine are more than mere symbols. As Article XXVIII, Of the Lord's Supper, states, "the Bread which we break is a partaking of the body of Christ; and likewise the Cup of Blessing is a partaking of the Blood of Christ."

Amen.

Mark 9:14–32, March 8th, 2015

Last week we had the 'mountain top' experience: Jesus' transfiguration. If you'd like to turn to that passage, you can remind yourself of it; you'll find it on p. 978 in the church Bibles, Mk. ch. 9, beginning at v. 2. Jesus is there, along with Moses and Elijah. And Jesus' appearance is miraculously transformed, he is transfigured. Peter, James and John get to experience a vision of Jesus' glory. Wow, as Sean would put it on our sign!

Last week I shared from memory a Peanuts cartoon. Then, via the miracle of the Internet, I thought to look up said cartoon, so this week I can give it you verbatim. Lucy: "Sometimes I get discouraged". Charlie Brown: "Well, Lucy, life does have its ups and downs, you know ... " This bit of wisdom sets Lucy off on a three-frame spin. "But why? Why should it?! Why can't my life be all 'ups'? If I want all 'ups', why can't I have them? Why can't I just move from one 'up' to another 'up'? Why can't I just go from an 'up' to an 'upper-up'? I don't want any 'downs'! I just want 'ups' and 'ups' and 'ups'!" At which point Charlie Brown retreats muttering, "I can't stand it."

We may feel the temptation to 'be a Lucy'. We want our Christian experience to be up and up and up. And there are various ways people have attempted this. For example retreating into a monastery. Or how about Simon Stylites? He spent 37 years on top of a pillar, eventually coming down on September 2nd 459. But whereas Jesus tells his disciples that they are not to be "of the world", we are still called to be in it.

And so, with Jesus, Peter, James and John descend from the mountain, v. 9. Now this section of Mark is something of a rollercoaster ride. At 8:29 Peter says of Jesus, "You are the Christ." That's a high point. But then Peter tries to dissuade Jesus from taking the pathway to the cross, earning the rebuke from Jesus, "Get behind me, Satan!" A low point. Then there's the high point of the Transfiguration. What comes next?

Last week I drew a comparison between the Transfiguration and Moses meeting with God on Mount Sinai. What did he discover when he returned from the mountain? It wasn't good. In his absence, the Israelites had made and were worshipping a golden calf. His brother Aaron gives the lamest of explanations: "they gave me the gold, and I threw it into the fire, and out came this calf!" Ex. 32:24.

What do Jesus, Peter James and John discover when they meet up with the other disciples again? There are the "teachers of the law" and true to form, they're arguing, about all they're good at. There's an evil spirit, v. 17: Satan is making his presence felt again. And there's unbelief: "O unbelieving generation," Jesus says, v. 19. This is the world as it is. This is the world that needs Jesus' presence, and us as his representatives. This is the world he willingly descends into.

And we see the difference Jesus' presence makes. V. 20: "When the spirit saw Jesus, it immediately threw the boy into a convulsion. He fell to the ground and rolled around, foaming at the mouth." We shouldn't be surprised at this. The spirit recognised that in Jesus it had met its match and it reacts accordingly.

The father of the boy had told Jesus, "I asked your disciples to drive out the spirit, but they could not." That experience may well have shaken the father's belief. And so his request of Jesus is somewhat muted. V. 22: "if you can do anything, take pity on us and help us." " 'If you can?' said Jesus. 'Everything is possible for him who believes.' "

I remember someone in my last pastorate coming up to me over coffee with a challenging question. Actually, it's rather refreshing when this happens, when someone asks something that shows they've been engaging with the service. It was in a beautiful, perhaps even somewhat cute, English parish church dating from the eleventh century and there couldn't have been more than a dozen worshippers, not bad for a village of 175. But even in such a setting, people can have challenging questions that need to be answered.

The service had been Prayer Book Morning Prayer and the question was about the Prayer of St. Chrysostom. I was asked, "You've just said that 'when two or three are gathered together in thy Name thou wilt grant their requests.' How come I prayed for my relative and she didn't get well again?"

I must admit that whereas I welcome such challenges, I didn't feel totally prepared at that moment as the assembled group waited for the response of their Vicar. The best I could come up with was to refer to how the prayer continues: "Fulfil now, O Lord, the desires and petitions of thy servants, as may be most expedient for them; granting us in this world knowledge of thy truth, and in the world to come life everlasting."

I don't think that St. Chrysostom, who was quoting from Jesus' words in Mt. 18:19, intended us to believe that we would always get what we ask for. The key words are that our approach to God as supplicants is that of servants to a master. And the master or lord knows what is "expedient"; he knows what the best answer is. And so we go on to request "knowledge of thy truth", the ability to discern and accept the answer God gives. The good news is that we look forward to "life everlasting" in the "world to come." That is when there will be no more suffering, and our 'mountain top' experience will be perpetual as we are able to bask in God's glory for ever.

Whereas, as Jesus says, "Everything is possible for him who believes"; this doesn't mean that there's nothing we can't do or have. That, remarkably, is what some teach. I came across it whilst living in Sydney. People influenced by New Age teaching that you have a god inside you. If you somehow realise that and harness it, then anything can be accomplished. As I said, I find it remarkable that people should think such a thing because it just so obviously isn't the case. What is true is that someone who has faith in Jesus won't put any limit on what God can do. "Nothing is impossible with God", Lk. 1:37.

The boy's father responds to Jesus with words that surely have resonated with many down the ages. They certainly resonate with me and, I'd suggest, with all of us at one time or another if we're honest. V. 24: "I do believe; help me overcome my unbelief." That is a prayer that God will answer. I believe that anyone who genuinely comes to God, with the earnest request for belief, will receive that gift. That has been my experience, dating from when I prayed a prayer of Christian commitment and basically said to God, now it's over to you!

Before telling us of Jesus rebuking the evil spirit and its coming out of the boy, Mark mentions that Jesus "saw that a crowd was running to the scene," v. 25. Do you realise what this means? Jesus had taken the boy away from them in order to deal with him. The casting out of the spirit wasn't a spectacle for all to observe.

Then Jesus went indoors and, v. 28, "his disciples asked him privately, 'why couldn't we drive it out?' He replied, 'This kind can come out only by prayer.' " The implication is that what the disciples had lacked was an attitude of prayer. If we think back to ch. 6, v. 12, we read there that the Twelve "went out and preached that people should repent. They drove out many demons."

What has gone wrong? My conjecture is that 'professionalism' had set in. The disciples had forgotten the source of the power by which they were able to minister. Hence they had forgotten the vitality need of prayer for them to achieve the task.

I think back to a ministry review with my bishop back in my first year of ordained ministry. I foolishly said that I found funerals 'easy'. The bishop, in the episcopal equivalent of a ton of bricks, reminded me not to take my ministry too casually.

Even Moses got it wrong. Moses had struck the rock at Horeb and water had come out for the people to drink, Ex. 17:6. Forty years on at Kadesh he again performed this miracle. But this time it was with what may be described as bad grace: "Listen, you rebels, must we bring you water out of this rock?" Num. 20:10. Professionalism had set in, causing the Lord to say to Moses and Aaron, "Because you did not trust in me enough to honour me as holy in the sight of the Israelites, you will not bring this community into the land I give them", Num. 20:12.

Jesus had not been with the disciples when they had tried to drive out the spirit; he had been up the mountain. But his power would have been with them if they had prayed. Prayer is vital. If we are going to achieve anything at Holy Trinity, prayer is vital. If we try without it, we will fail, just as the disciples had.

I attended the Evangelical Anglican Leaders Conference in January 1995. The Archbishop of Canterbury gave the closing address. Nothing strange in that, you might think. The remarkable aspect was that the conference was held in Westminster Chapel, London, and George Carey was standing in the pulpit formerly occupied by the minister of that church, Dr. Martyn Lloyd-Jones, who in 1966 had issued his call for evangelicals to leave the Church of England; sound familiar? George brought some levity to the occasion, by reaching down in the pulpit and showing us a rather old-fashioned looking telephone. "I always wondered what the secret of Dr. Lloyd-Jones' ministry was," he told us, "the hotline!" In 1992 the Staler Brothers sang the gospel song 'Turn Your Radio On', get in touch with God. Prayer is our hotline to God.

Do you pray? This whole service is an opportunity for prayer. I've sometimes been told, you didn't pray for someone or something in the service, which you should have done. Maybe so. But there's nothing to stop anyone of you from praying nonetheless. I commend to you our monthly prayer meetings as vital. The measure of a church is when we see opportunities for prayer as a priority, rather going to a prayer meeting than to a place of entertainment. I commend to you daily personal prayer. Do you use our weekly prayer sheet and supplement it with your own written list of people and situations to pray for?

V. 30: "They left that place and passed through Galilee. Jesus did not want anyone to know where they were, because he was teaching his disciples. He said to them, 'The Son of Man is going to be betrayed into the hands of men. They will kill him, and after three days he will rise.' But they did not understand what he meant and were afraid to ask him about it."

Again we've got Jesus alone with his disciples and not wanting others to know. He didn't want events to overtake them before he'd been able to prepare the disciples through teaching them. And they still had much to learn. Peter had struggled when Jesus had talked about his death and resurrection in ch. 8. In ch. 9 v. 10, the disciples had discussed "what 'rising from the dead' meant."

Perhaps it's too much to expect them to understand until they had experienced. But then they experienced and they understood. And this too must be part of our experience and understanding of Jesus. His death and resurrection must be the foundation of our relationship with him through prayer and our ministry in his name.

We have advantages over the disciples as they were in Mk. ch. 9. We have the complete Bible as testimony to what occurred. Added to which are two thousand years of church history and in particular the witness of our Reformation forebears. May our prayer be "I do believe; help me overcome my unbelief" so that ours may not be described as an "unbelieving generation".

Amen.

Mark 9:33–50, March 15th, 2015

You'll find our passage on p. 979 in the church Bibles, Mk. ch. 9 beginning at v. 33. I invite you to turn to it. Jesus and the disciples have travelled through Galilee on the way to Capernaum. And there's been conversation en route. What have they been talking about? Maybe they've been considering what's been going on? What was that?

If we look back, we see that Jesus had taken the disciples apart because he wished to teach them. He put on a mini course in Christian basics, a study day if you will. The topic was as basic as it gets, what lies at the heart of Christianity: his death and resurrection. That's what he wanted them to know about. The fact that he allocates time and space for this is a pretty good indication of the importance he attaches to this teaching.

We know that the subject of Jesus' death and resurrection was at that time something of a hot potato for the disciples and that they were having difficulty working out what it was about. We know that from Peter's reaction when Jesus first told them that he was going to die: ch. 8, v. 32. And from 9:10, when Peter, James and John discussed "what 'rising from the dead' meant."

Knowing that the disciples were struggling with this, and having just been at a teaching session with Jesus about it, did the disciples take the opportunity of the road journey to discuss it further? No. In fact it's worse than that. Look back at v. 32. Not only did they "not understand what he meant [they] were afraid to ask him about it."

You don't understand something that you feel you ought to understand. But rather than admitting to your ignorance, you don't want to appear stupid. And so you don't ask. I think that Christians of long standing, long-time church members, can suffer from this syndrome. It can inhibit people from attending courses. But we are all called not to be students who will complete a period of training, but disciples engaged in life-long learning.

But perhaps the reason the disciples didn't want to talk about it is that subjects such as the crucifixion can be regarded as rather dark. I mentioned last Good Friday a church in my home city of Birmingham, where parents asked for a crucifix to be removed, saying that it scared the children. I've come across the attitude in church circles that want to talk about only the nice bits of Christianity, love and light, not death and sin.

So what was it that the disciples were talking about as they travelled to Capernaum? That one subject that we can all agree is our favourite: ourselves! But again, it gets worse. Twice we're told, vv. 33 and 34, that they hadn't just talked, they'd argued. Their discussion of themselves and each other hadn't been affirming of the other; it had been competitive: "Who was the greatest"?

It's remarkable: take Jesus out of the equation and sin creeps in. The backbiting starts and self-aggrandisement. You might think their thoughts would have been captivated by Jesus. They were in his presence and they'd experienced and he'd told them so many remarkable things. But no, they'd argued and indulged in self-promotion and putting others down. We should compare ourselves only with Christ, not with others.

What about our thoughts and conversations? What is the buzz over coffee? Is it about Jesus? Is it self-abasing and looking out for others? Or is it centred on a grievance, something or someone not to my liking?

The subject of the "pursuit of happiness" cropped up in our Re-Frame course. It's part of the American Declaration of Independence. On Friday I saw parts of the movie *Groundhog Day*, rather silly, but fun. A rather cynical and miserable TV reporter learns the lesson that happiness is gained through making others happy. It's a by-product if you will: the irony is, pursue it for yourself and it's likely to elude you.

V. 37: "Whoever welcomes one of these little children in my name welcomes me." This is a practical illustration of what Jesus has just told the disciples: "If anyone wants to be first, he must be the very last, and the servant of all" [v. 35]. A child is a natural example of someone who is young in the faith, a young Christian who needs to be built up and encouraged.

I remember being told by someone senior to me in the Church that I had to "earn my stripes." I didn't think that was a particularly Christian attitude and I still don't! Perhaps those who have been in the Church for some time need to continually learn the lesson that Paul knew: I am what I am "by the grace of God", I Cor. 15:10.

What is your attitude to newcomers to our church? Is it that they've got to "earn their stripes", their place among us? Has your self-worth somehow become tied up with performing a particular task so that you're unwilling to share it with someone else or help someone to do something?

In another place, someone was bemoaning people who had left the church. When I pointed to others who had joined, the sentiment was that they're not one of us. They're not my friends whom I miss, or they're not going to give as much as so and so did. And so we seek after those who have left at the expense of those who seek to join.

We need to hear and heed Jesus' words in v. 42: "If anyone causes one of these little ones who believe in me to sin, it would be better for him to be thrown into the sea with a large millstone tied around his neck." We need to welcome and build-up the newcomer, the young Christian. To include them and embrace them for who they are.

V. 38: " 'Teacher,' said John, 'we saw a man driving out demons in your name and we told him to stop, because he was not one of us.' " We need to see this is the light of what has occurred: the disciples had previously been unable to drive out an evil spirit, v. 18. Now here's someone who's "not one of us" who is able to do so. And the disciples don't like it. Again, is this a matter of pride, standing on status as the chosen few?

I find clergy gatherings interesting. On the surface we're very polite to each other, of course. But underneath, there's often a competitive element. It's interesting how the size of one's congregation tends to crop up. I'll admit that I used to quite like those websites, often for an Episcopal church, that seemingly brag about what's on offer, fantastic music and the like. I found the enthusiasm quite endearing.

But I see the danger of this culture of 'success' which says come to us because we're so much bigger and better and we'll give you more of what you want. God doesn't call us to be successful; he calls us to be faithful. Perhaps websites should be more honest about how we struggle with that! The key is, "in my name." This phrase encapsulates that we are doing something on Jesus' behalf and through his power, his Spirit. Whether someone or a church is doing this or not, is the criterion by which we should measure.

We've seen how a concentration on myself and my needs can supplant Jesus. Jesus uses metaphor to urge us, in somewhat graphic terms, to be aware of ways in which we can become distracted. He refers to the hand, foot and eye as symbolic of our actions. The message is, be aware of how you might be led astray. And do something about avoiding this.

Giving up something for Lent is a popular practice, or not so popular, if it happens to be something you like! I'm not particularly into giving up things for Lent, but I am for avoiding the things that might lead us astray from our walk with Jesus. And these will be different things for different people. I don't have a television: I don't find what's on it helpful and I don't miss it! Something to consider: how about switching off the television, at least for the remainder of Lent? There are only three weeks to go.

The Greek word translated as "hell" is in this instance "*Gehenna*", a place of fire and purging. It's not somewhere one would want to go and there's no need to do so. It is only if someone avoids Jesus, bypassing him, that *Gehenna* is likely to be his destination. The point of the things that might lead one there is that they lead us away from Jesus. If we stay close to Jesus as his disciples, we can be sure that *Gehenna* is not for us.

As Jesus' disciples, staying close to him is a life-long journey of getting to know him better. We do this along with others, not in a competitive spirit, but in a spirit of servanthood, looking out for one another. We measure ourselves by how well we know Jesus as our crucified and resurrected Lord. And we seek to see others with the same graciousness that Jesus sees us, as we serve one another in his name.

Amen.

Mark 10:1–16, March 22nd, 2015

Last week I mentioned that the subject of Jesus' death and resurrection was for the disciples, who at that time had still to experience those events, something of a hot potato. This week Mark has served up a hot potato for us to deal with, something that is a big issue in our context, that of divorce. I'm glad, I think, that my policy of sequential reading through Mark's Gospel account doesn't allow us to dodge what the Bible has to say on the topic.

I'm aware that I'm addressing this as someone who has never been married. I can't fully enter into the experience of what it means to be married, or to have marital difficulties, or go through a divorce. But that's true for many issues that life throws at us. It shouldn't prevent us from empathising with others and bringing truths from God's Word to bear. Indeed, sometimes people need someone else to speak from outside of a situation to enable them to hear what God has to say.

Let's turn to our passage which you'll find on p. 979 in the church Bibles, Mk. ch. 10. V. 1: "crowds of people came to [Jesus], and as was his custom, he taught them." A teaching ministry was important to Jesus and it should be important to his Church. And he taught the "crowds". Our message is relevant to all, those within our fellowship and those we seek to reach outside. We need to be aware of that as we frame what it is we seek to say; to enable that which is most important to be heard and received. We say at the beginning of our [Contemporary] Worship that we seek "to hear and receive God's holy word" and, by extension, to enable others to do so.

V. 2: "Some Pharisees came and tested [Jesus]." Part of divorce being a hot-button issue is that it can be used as a stick with which to beat the Church. All the more reason for us to know what we believe about the topic and why we believe it.

V. 3: Jesus replied, "What did Moses command you?" Jesus refers to Scripture. This is all the more remarkable given who Jesus is. He could have just spoken and that would have been God's Word to us. Indeed, in my NIV Study Bible, Jesus' words are printed in red. But he chooses to refer to Scripture and that's what we need to do as well.

Jesus had an advantage over us as many of those he spoke to, and certainly the Pharisees, knew the words of Scripture, so he was able to elicit a scriptural response from those who questioned him. And the Pharisees would have acknowledged the authority of Scripture, something again that we may have to battle for in our context. But there's a difference between knowing a text and understanding it and putting it into practice. Part of this involves seeing any text in the context of what the rest of the Bible has to say, which for us as Christians involves the New Testament as well as the Old.

Divorce and remarriage were allowed by the Old Testament. The text the Pharisees quote is Deut. ch. 24. It mentions two grounds for a man to divorce his wife: if she "becomes displeasing to him" and if "he finds something indecent about her." This led to two schools of practice within Judaism. There were those who allowed 'easy divorce': the wife no longer pleased her husband, so he wrote "a certificate of divorce" and she was dispensed with. Against this view were those who said that divorce was allowed only on the grounds of adultery.

Jesus now introduces the concept of hardened hearts; v. 5: "It was because your hearts were hard that Moses wrote you this law." Does this mean that for followers of Christ the dispensation that Moses provided no longer applies? I think what Jesus says could mean this only if we believe that 'hardened hearts' no longer exist. But we know, from our studies in Mark so far, that that is not the case. Mk. 3:5: "[Jesus] looked around at them in anger, and deeply distressed at their stubborn hearts"; 6:52: "they had not understood about the loaves; their hearts were hardened"; 8:17: "Do you still not see or understand? Are your hearts hardened?"

The term 'hardness of heart' may be thought of as being slightly quaint. Because of this, perhaps we hear it and brush over it. But it's really important and lies at the heart of Christian discipleship. What does it mean? To what does it refer? It means, are you open to the things of God? What is the guiding principle in your life? Is it yourself, your needs and wants? Or are you willing to be open to and accept what God says, what God wants? Do you seek to discern and obey God's Word in your life? Who's in control, you or God? I hope you can see that whether a person's heart is hardened or not is foundational to understanding Christianity.

The fact that the word "permitted" is used in v. 4 is an indication that whereas divorce is allowed, it is not desired. Behind this lies an affirmation of marriage and an understanding of what marriage is. Jesus refers to creation, v. 6: "at the beginning of creation God 'made them male and female.' " We're talking about a foundational matter here, going back to God's intention in creation. Jesus continues quoting from Gen. 2:27: "For this reason a man will leave his father and mother and be united to his wife, and the two will become one flesh" [vv. 7,8]. At v. 9, Jesus speaks words that are part of our Anglican Marriage service, when the minister joins the hands of bride and groom: "What God has joined together, let man not separate."

As marriage is so important in God's eyes, alongside taking a view on divorce, we also need to consider why marriages break down and what can be done to prevent this. The elements that contribute toward a good marriage are those that constitute living with a heart open to God. Whom are both parties putting first? Is it themselves? We're back to having a hardened heart. Being open to God also involves being open to the other person, being willing to put that person before oneself. Communicating. Being willing to say sorry. How often does someone admit he or she was in the wrong too late, when the damage is done? Marriage must be a subject of prayer. And that means the couple praying but also those who surround them: their family and friends, the Church. We all bear responsibility for supporting those who are married.

But nonetheless, we know that hardened hearts persist in the world as it is. And so for Christians, divorce is permitted in two instances. One is "marital unfaithfulness", adultery, and this is made clear by Jesus in Mt. 19:9. The other is mentioned by Paul in I Cor. 7:15. It concerns a believer married to an unbeliever. If a non-Christian leaves his or her Christian partner, then Paul says the Christian "is not bound". I interpret this as meaning he or she is free to remarry.

We read that the disciples asked Jesus about this matter when they were alone. Vv. 11 and 12: "He answered, 'Anyone who divorces his wife and marries another woman commits adultery against her. And if she divorces her husband and marries another man, she commits adultery.'" I think it's important to note exactly how Jesus phrases this. He refers specifically to a man or woman actively divorcing his or her spouse. This introduces the concept of 'the guilty party'. The other person is 'the innocent party' in the divorce. And such a person is, in my opinion, free to remarry.

I recall back in 1982 a school-friend telling me that he would like to live with someone before marrying her but that he wouldn't do so. The remarkable thing is that he didn't say this because he was a Christian; he was in fact an atheist and hadn't even been baptised. And also he was extremely bright, which one might associate with being a free-thinker. The reason he gave for not living together was that it was 'socially unacceptable'. How things have changed!

When ministering in England from 2004 to 2013, I worked on the assumption that those who brought their children for baptism were unmarried: the baptism of the first child often seemed to take the place of a marriage celebration. And that those who presented themselves for marriage would have children, who often had a rôle in the marriage service.

This is the context in which we have to seek to minister and engage with people. I had a telephone conversation with a parishioner yesterday when I mentioned that I was to tackle the subject of divorce in my sermon. He remarked that the problem was that the Church sought to fit in with society rather than following what the Bible taught. I countered by saying that I hoped that I put the Bible's teaching first, but that we also had to be aware of our context. We're back to trying to help people 'hear and receive' what God says. The vital part is seeking opportunities to 'soften people's hearts' to enable them to do so.

Until 2002 the Church of England did not allow divorcees to remarry in church. Then things changed, but the onus lay with the Rector whether or not he was going to allow this: thanks a lot! While I was a curate, I did not have a say; it was the practice of the Rectors I served under to remarry divorcees and so I had to do so. Then I became Vicar of The Cranmer Group and the buck stopped with me. The problem was that my predecessor had remarried divorcees and I inherited bookings for people who were divorced. And all the other churches in my deanery married divorcees.

And so I decided to do so as well. I followed the guidelines laid down by the Church of England. I wouldn't conduct the marriage if the new relationship had been the cause of the breakdown of the former marriage. And I wouldn't remarry someone who had been divorced more than once.

But nonetheless, I got in trouble with one of my faithful church members. To her credit, she took the opportunity to talk privately with me about her misgivings rather than talking behind my back. This gave me the opportunity to share my thoughts on the biblical material we've been looking at today. And I also added this. In the Church of England, I was duty bound by law to conduct a marriage if neither person had been divorced, regardless of however many prior non-marital relationships there may have been. Given this, it seemed inconsistent to discriminate against a person whose one previous attempt at a relationship had been in the context of a marriage that had failed.

I seem to recall that the breakdown of relationships of the girlfriend/boyfriend variety used to be a staple source of material for pop songs; in 1962 Neil Sedaka sang 'Breaking up is Hard to Do'.

It may be just that I'm out of touch with contemporary pop music culture, which I am! But I get the feeling that this theme isn't as prevalent nowadays. Is it because breakups, now including marriage, are not 'news' any more?

But the fact is that the pain inflicted by breakups, particularly of marriage, is just as real, even if it's not sung about. And I'm particularly concerned about the effect of marriage breakdown on children: if ever there was an 'innocent party' it is they. I've heard it said that the extent of marriage breakdown and divorce that we're experiencing is one of the greatest 'social experiments' ever. And who knows where it will lead for the children affected?

I've put on the church's Facebook page an article from yesterday's *Globe and Mail*. In it, Margaret Wente writes, "mountains of evidence show that the breakdown of traditional families ... has been terrible for children and society." She ends on a somewhat plaintive note: "What's to be done? No one knows ... let's back marriage. But how, pray tell, are we supposed to do that? David Brooks of *The New York Times* speaks wistfully of a 'moral revival' that might occur through 'organic communal effort, with voices from everywhere saying gently: This we praise. This we don't.' But who is 'we'? And who's listening? There must be other ideas out there. If only I had a clue what they might be."[ii]

My response to Margaret Wente's questions is to say maybe the Church and the Bible have something to say on this matter, if only people would listen. We're back to the subject of hardness of hearts. Do we seek to discern and obey God's Word? The evidence Margaret Wente points to indicates that the problems start when we don't.

It is fitting that our passage moves from discussion of divorce to that of children. V. 13: "People were bringing little children to Jesus to have him touch them, but the disciples rebuked them. When Jesus saw this, he was indignant." We need to recall that in v. 37 of the previous chapter Jesus had told the disciples, "Whoever welcomes one of these little children in my name welcomes me." Talk about hardness of heart: the disciples appeared to have forgotten Jesus' teaching already!

I've heard it said that children are 'the church of tomorrow'; they're not: they're the church of today! One of the ways in which Vancouver is different from where I've ministered previously is that many of my fellow evangelicals are in churches such as the Mennonites and Christian & Missionary Alliance and, of course the Baptists, that do not practice infant baptism. I respect their stance, although I do not agree with it.

In the Anglican Church we baptise infants on the basis of the faith of the parents. This equates baptism with the rite of circumcision in the Old Testament. Baptism is a sign not of personal profession of faith by the person being baptised, that we pray will come later, but of God's graciousness toward that person. From the moment of baptism, the child is a member of the Church, to be brought up and nurtured within God's covenant.

The Church of England's liturgy of 1980 puts it this way: "Children who are too young to profess the Christian faith are baptized on the understanding that they are brought up as Christians within the family of the Church. As they grow up, they need the help and encouragement of that family, so that they learn to be faithful in public worship and private prayer, to live by trust in God, and come to confirmation." And confirmation provides the opportunity for public profession of faith.

I see this pattern of practice as expressive of Jesus' words and actions. V. 14: "Let the little children come to me and do not hinder them, for the kingdom of God belongs to such as these." V. 16: "And he took the children in his arms, put his hands on them and blessed them."

Jesus also says, v. 15, "I tell you the truth, anyone who will not receive the kingdom of God like a little child will never enter it." Anyone: that includes you and me! Karl Barth, as well as having a fine Christian name spelt with a 'K', was probably the greatest theologian of the twentieth century. His magnum opus, *Church Dogmatics*, extended to thirteen volumes.

During a US lecture tour in 1962 he spoke in the Rockefeller Chapel at the University of Chicago. A student asked him if he could summarise his whole life's work in theology in a sentence. Barth replied, "Yes, I can. In the words of a song I learned at my mother's knee: 'Jesus loves me, this I know, for the Bible tells me so.' "

And so we return to our theme of softened versus hardened hearts. Karl Barth, for all his greatness as a theologian, knew that at the heart of Christianity is a simple childlike trust in the promises of God. In fact, it's that knowledge that, to my mind, was a vital prerequisite to his being a great theologian. As the Church of England puts it: "to live by trust in God".

Amen.

Mark 10:17–31, March 29th, 2015

I'll start with an apology. I know today is Palm Sunday but this isn't going to be a particularly Palm Sunday-ish sermon. Instead, we're going to have the last in our current series of sermons on Mark's gospel account before we break for Easter. Part of my reason is that I want to refer to last week's sermon about children whilst it's still fresh in your minds. But try to look at it from my point of view: there's only so much you can say about a donkey year in and year out! And I am going to try to squeeze in a camel, so look out for it!

May I invite you to turn to our passage; it's on p. 980 in the church Bibles, Mk. ch. 10, beginning at v. 17? You'll see that the NIV has headed the passage "The Rich Young Man." We know that he was rich from Mark's account; v. 22: "he had great wealth." The fact that he was young is gleaned from the parallel account in Matthew, and Luke describes him as a "ruler".

He appeared to have it all. He was either born wealthy or else had 'made good' at a young age. He was a person of status and authority. We're not told so, but let's throw in good looks and intelligence. He may have been a very eligible bachelor, the type of person we'd love to have as a member of our church!

We're told in v. 17 that he "ran up to [Jesus]." We might not think anything of the fact that he ran. After all, we see plenty of young people running about Vancouver, if only running to catch a bus or to cross the road before the lights change. Vancouver casual attire is well suited to this, quite possibly incorporating 'running shoes' as a matter of fashion. But you've got to imagine this man in sandals having to hitch up his flowing robes, quite a sight. And running just wasn't on for a person of status. Think of the father that ran to meet his prodigal son: it had been demeaning for him to do so.

The Pharisees in v. 2 had asked Jesus a question in order to 'test' him: they were trying to catch him out. But the means of approach of the young man, "[falling] on his knees before [Jesus]", speaks of the genuineness and sincerity of his question: "what must I do to inherit eternal life?"

When I was a curate in Chester-le-Street, I was asked to visit a woman in hospital. Jean was dying of a brain tumour. She had no previous contact with the Church; but she wanted to speak to a clergyman because she knew she was dying and wanted to know what would happen next. What a privilege it was to minister to her; to be able to share passages from the Bible, such as this, with her. I was later asked to take her funeral and was able to minister to her family.

My time with Jean stands out because so often it feels as if clergy are regarded, and act, as just second-rate social workers. Or else we're administrators, keeping the show on the road. But Jean was a woman in extremis asking the sort of question that I came into ministry to answer.

Jesus' initial response to the man is to list the last six of the Ten Commandments, the ones to do with our relationships with other people. I can only imagine that the man's heart leapt at hearing this, thinking he was on a 'home run'. The word in v. 20 that the NIV translates "declared", *ephē*, means 'to say assertively'; " 'Teacher,' he declared, 'all these I have kept since I was a boy.' "

When our service is Holy Communion, we hear read either the Ten Commandments, as today, or Jesus' summary of the Law contained in Mk. ch. 12. In a sense, we need to hear both; it isn't an either-or. We might consider it possible to keep the six commandments Jesus quotes to the man; although Jesus raises the bar by saying in Mt. 5 that "anyone who looks at a woman lustfully has already committed adultery with her in his heart"; and anyone who's a parent may dispute what 'honouring your father and mother' entails.

But Jesus' summary, which is actually direct quotations from Deut. 6:5 and Lev. 19:18 in the Old Testament, encapsulates both the six commandments relating to other people, and the four that precede them, that directly relate to God. In each case "love" is the first word, and regarding God, Jesus states that this is to involve all our heart, soul, mind and strength.

I spoke about the state of our hearts last week, whether they are hardened or softened or broken in our attitude toward God. We hear the commandments read, yes, to remind us of them and that they still apply, but not that we should feel good about having successfully kept them. For if we see them not just as a matter of outward actions, but involving our hearts and, vitally, love, if we're honest, we know that we have failed. And so we say, "Lord have mercy". The purpose of hearing them is to drive us to Jesus as the only one capable of fulfilling their requirements in their entirety.

When Jesus says to the man, v. 21, "Go, sell everything you have and give to the poor" it's because he's discerned where the man's heart lies. And he's discerned the blockage that lies between the man and God. The man isn't able to love God with all his heart, soul, mind and strength because of his preoccupation with wealth.

When Jesus tells the man this, it's like a doctor prescribing medicine that may taste unpleasant but is necessary to restore someone to health. We're told that "Jesus looked at him and loved him" [v. 21]. Oh just to have Jesus look at one, but also to feel his love. Sometimes ministry involves, as Paul puts it, "speaking the truth in love," Ephesians 4:15. This may not always be well received, people's faces may fall, or worse! But it is necessary, for the sake of the truth and for the wellbeing of the person concerned.

The man had asked about "eternal life." Jesus' response is to call the man to address the blockage his wealth imposes, and then to say "come, follow me." Earlier, in v. 18, Jesus had said to him, "Why do you call me good? ... No one is good — except God alone." Jesus isn't saying it's wrong to call him "good" — in fact it's exactly right to do so — the question is, why? And the answer is because Jesus is God and that's why the path to eternal life must involve following him.

Jesus has been addressing the man and his situation directly. The prescription he gives, "to sell everything that you have", is specific to him: we don't find Jesus saying this elsewhere. But now, v. 23, Jesus talks more generally and addresses his disciples: "How hard it is for the rich to enter the kingdom of God!" We're told that "The disciples were amazed at his words", v. 24.

I'll admit to being in awe of some people, the rich and famous. I was at the service in Westminster Abbey for the commencement of the Church of England's General Synod. There were two people between me and the aisle. As we sang the processional hymn, there, all of a sudden, was the Queen. I could have reached over and touched her. The sense of awe I felt makes me think that if I had to speak to her, my mouth would open and shut, but my mind would have no control over what came out! I think this lies behind the disciples saying to each other, "Who then can be saved?" v. 26. Are they buying into the notion that wealth should be able to provide some sort of 'fast track'? Let's remember what Billy Graham said after preaching before the Queen at Sandringham: "I'm always preaching before the King of Kings and Lord of Lords."

Jesus isn't saying that it's impossible for a rich man to enter the kingdom of God; he says that it's hard for him to do so. And his illustration of a camel going through the eye of a needle reinforces this point. The illustration can be understood two ways; I think both are legitimate and say the same thing.

One is to understand that the 'eye of the needle' refers to a particular gateway through the walls of Jerusalem. The gate was narrow, such that a heavily laden camel, weighed down with belongings, would have difficulty passing. The other way is to take the illustration literally: it's obviously impossible for a camel to pass through an actual eye of a needle.

Incidentally, does anyone know the nickname for the Bank of England? The Old Lady of Threadneedle Street. It's interesting that the bank should be located on a street that makes allusion to this biblical imagery.

How do we hold together the two interpretations of Jesus' illustration, one seeing it as hard but not impossible for the camel to pass, and the other as more definitely impossible? The answer is in what Jesus says in v. 27: "With man this is impossible, but not with God; all things are possible with God."

The man had asked, "What must I do to inherit eternal life?" Maybe he was a self-made man, used to getting things by his own efforts, by what he does. But that's never true of an inheritance. You inherit something through the action and will of someone else, the one who grants the inheritance. In the case of eternal life, that someone is God.

In v. 24, Jesus refers to the disciples as "Children." Last week we looked at v. 15, where Jesus said, "I tell you the truth, anyone who will not receive the kingdom of God like a little child will never enter it." Children are good at receiving gifts. There's none of the false modesty that adults put on — "no you shouldn't have" — children just rip off the paper eager to see what's inside. The kingdom of God can't be earned by what we do, it's received as a gift from God.

Jesus promises us blessing for faithfulness to him and the gospel: "a hundred times as much in this present age ... and in the age to come eternal life", v. 30. This has sometimes been construed as a 'prosperity gospel': "follow Jesus and you'll get rich." But it's hard to reconcile this with Jesus' overall emphasis against focussing on riches. As part of our sinful state we can fail to recognise what are in fact God's blessings, in the same way that he answers our prayers, but not necessarily in the ways we expect.

For the rich young man his wealth was a stumbling-block that needed to be addressed. That may be the case for us as well. Paul reminds us that "the love of money is a root of all kinds of evil", I Tim. 6:10. I remember a talk at the Christian Union when I was a student back in the 1980s. We were told to get used to tithing, giving a tenth of what we have to the Church, while we still had little as students, as it would get progressively harder to maintain this as we gained more and more. All of us are materially rich when compared with people from past ages or people currently living in some parts of the world. However much we give, we need to remember that all that we have comes from God and is in fact God's, and so must be used wisely.

Eternal life, entry into the kingdom of God, isn't something that we can earn. It is to be received as a gift, as with any inheritance. Jesus' concern is where our heart is. Do you "Love the Lord your God with all your heart"?; do you have no other gods but him? Or is your heart preoccupied with money or something else? If it is, you need to do something about this. Be assured that by doing so you will gain far more than you will ever lose.

Amen.

Mark 10:32–45, June 21st, 2015

Today we resume our study of Mark's gospel account. We've been working our way progressively through Mark, in six-week blocks, since starting in March last year. I hope that you've found this approach helpful. I certainly have; it has informed my preaching. This is actually the first time I've experienced this approach with one of the gospel accounts. And it's given me a fresh appreciation.

We tend to experience, and therefore think about, the gospels in a rather bitty way. And Mark's account is sometimes looked down upon: it's the shortest of the accounts, the most pithy, and the Greek in which it was originally written is the least sophisticated. What I've come to appreciate is the literary structure that Mark has applied. This is in no way to take away from the truthfulness of what he says. But he's telling a story with a message. And, in my opinion, he's remarkably effective at doing so.

At our Bible Study on Thursday, the question of the difference between the terms disciple and apostle arose. Disciples is used of Jesus' followers before his resurrection. It means a follower or pupil, one who is taught. It's used of the wide circle that followed Jesus, and also of the twelve disciples, his inner circle. The term apostle tends to be used after Jesus' resurrection and ascension. It means "one who is sent", a messenger, an ambassador. The disciples go from those who are being taught by Jesus, to those who are sent to teach others.

So in much of the gospels, the disciples are being taught by Jesus, in preparation for when he will no longer be with them in person, when he then sends them as apostles to teach others. And the teaching that we have about Jesus can be traced back to them. That's what's meant by the term Apostolic Succession, the passing on of the apostles' teaching, right down to our day. And that's why we say we are part of "one, holy, catholic, and apostolic Church."

Please turn to our passage, which you'll find on p. 980 of the church Bibles, Mk. ch. 10, beginning at v. 32. The NIV's editors provide the heading, "Jesus Again Predicts His Death." In the previous chapter, when coming down from the mount of Transfiguration, Jesus tells Peter, James and John that "the Son of Man must suffer much and be rejected", 9:12. And at ch. 8 v. 31, Jesus teaches the disciples that "the Son of Man ... must be killed and after three days rise again."

You may recall Peter's rather unfortunate response to this: "Peter took [Jesus] aside and began to rebuke him", 8:32. And in turn, Jesus rebukes Peter: "Get behind me Satan ... You do not have in mind the things of God, but the things of men", 8:33. There's a contrast between God's way of seeing things and doing things, and man's way of seeing and doing. And this continues in our passage, in ch. 10.

V. 32: "They were on their way up to Jerusalem, with Jesus leading the way, and the disciples were astonished, while those who followed were afraid." Jerusalem means bad news as far as the disciples are concerned, going into the lions' den. Yet Jesus boldly leads the way: he's not going to be deterred; just as he wasn't by Peter's, a.k.a. Satan's, rebuke in ch. 8.

" 'We are going up to Jerusalem,' he said, 'and the Son of Man will be betrayed to the chief priests and Teachers of the Law. They will condemn him to death and will hand him over to the Gentiles, who will mock him and spit on him, flog him and kill him. Three days later he will rise' " [10:33,34].

But this gives rise to what the NIV rather meekly refers to as "The Request of James and John." It's significant, I think, that the people concerned in these incidents, Peter, James and John, were the inner circle of the inner circle, those closest to Jesus. James and John were brothers and Jesus had given them the affectionate nickname *Boanerges*, Greek for "Sons of Thunder", Mk. 3:17.

It's this inner circle that Satan, wily fellow that he is, particularly seeks to attack. What James and John come up with is, to my mind, just as obviously satanically inspired as Peter's response in ch. 8. V. 35: " 'Teacher,' they said, 'we want you to do for us whatever we ask.' " I don't know about you, but my jaw drops when I hear those words.

In 1963, Robert Menzies, Prime Minister of Australia, quoted the poet Thomas Ford, in the Queen's presence: "I did but see her passing by, and yet I love her till I die." The expression on the Queen's face at that moment has been described as a cringe. For me, those words of James and John are such a cringe moment.

Yet, on the other hand, perhaps ne'er a truer word was spoken. Isn't what James and John articulate lurking behind many prayers? Ask a non-Christian about his attitude toward God, and you're likely to find something along the lines of, "we want you to do for us whatever we ask." And then we have to ask that question, rather more uncomfortably, of those in the Church and of ourselves. If God doesn't give us what we want, surely he's an unloving parent; or is it, in fact, that we're acting as a selfish child?

In 1993 the band Culture Beat, had a hit with the song 'Mr Vain', which includes the line, "I know what I want and I want it now", surely a mantra for our time. Jim Carey's 2003 film 'Bruce Almighty', is at once silly and profound. Bruce, the character played by Jim Carey — by the way, did you know that Jim Carey is Canadian? — thinks he can do a better job than God. And he's given the chance to prove it. He says yes to every prayer request en bloc. And chaos and misery abound as a result.

James and John's request, "Let one of us sit at your right hand and the other at your left in your glory", v. 37, is usually seen as a case of self-aggrandisement, which it is. But seen in tandem with Peter's rebuke of Jesus in ch. 8, I think they thought they knew better than Jesus, and they were seeking to save him from himself. I think they envisioned themselves as a phalanx of bodyguards, one on each side, able to provide wise counsel, and stop all this foolish talk of sacrificial death. Instead, their preference was, let's go straight to the glory.

What we have is akin to tectonic plates grinding against each other: God's way of suffering and service, recognising sin and dealing with it; and man's way, the way Satan would have us be: self-centred, self-serving, and blinkered regarding our sinfulness.

We're told in v. 41 that when the other ten disciples heard about James and John's request, they were indignant. I fear that their indignation was flavoured with, "Why didn't we think of that?" and "Why didn't we get in first?"

Jesus calls the disciples together, v. 42. When we read such a statement, we know he's about to say something that's particularly significant. What he teaches them is radically counter-cultural. He starts with what is the norm, what the disciples know to be the case: "those who are regarded as rulers of the Gentiles lord it over them, and their high officials exercise authority over them."

Jesus' repetition of "over them", "lord it over them", "exercise authority over them", is significant. To give you some idea of what's involved, the same Greek word is used in Acts 19:16 for when a man with an evil spirit "overpowered" the seven sons of Sceva. We're told that "He gave them such a beating that they ran out of the house naked and bleeding."

The turning-point in what Jesus tells the disciples comes at the beginning of v. 43, when he says, "Not so with you." I hear echoes of what Paul writes in Rom. ch. 6: "What shall we say, then? Shall we go on sinning so that grace may increase? By no means!"

Jesus continues, "whoever wants to become great among you must be your servant, and whoever wants to be first must be slave of all." Again, look for the repetition: "with you", "among you", actually the same words in the Greek: *en hymin*, among you. It's not enough to think, "I've served in the past, that ought to be enough." The Christian calling is one of constant ongoing service, here and now.

Jesus says, you know about the way of the world, the way of man, the way Satan would have us act and be. He goes on to tell us, it shall not be so among you; you are to follow God's way, a way of service and sacrifice; a counter-cultural way that goes against our sinful inclinations.

Why are we to do this? Jesus doesn't tell us to do something he isn't willing to do himself. V. 45: "For even the Son of Man did not come to be served, but to serve, and to give his life as a ransom for many."

Jesus told James and John, "You will drink the cup I drink and be baptised with the baptism I am baptised with," v. 39. James was to be the first of the Apostles to die a martyr's death, Acts 12:2. John, having suffered the loss of his brother, was the last of the Apostles to die; in lonely exile for his faith, on the Roman penal colony island of Patmos.

The first Christians were known as followers of "the Way", Acts 9:2. I see a parallel in the disciples being "on their way up to Jerusalem, with Jesus leading the way." After Jesus' rebuke of Peter in ch. 8, he "called the crowd to him along with the disciples and said: 'If anyone would come after me, he must deny himself and take up his cross and follow me", Mk. 8:34.

The Christian path can only be one that leads to the cross. A way of service and sacrifice. It's the only way that deals effectively with our sin and that can save us from our inclination for being self-serving, and self-aggrandising. And it's through belief in Jesus' sacrifice on the cross, and following his way of self-abasement, that glory is to be found.

Amen.

Mark 10:46–52, June 28th, 2015

I had a conversation with David on Friday about how the 1662 Book of Common Prayer makes no provision for hymns in addition to the liturgy. No hymns, as we know them, were sung in the Church of England, before their introduction through the ministry of John and Charles Wesley, the founders of Methodism.

Things came to a head in 1819, when the Revd. Thomas Cotterill, perpetual Curate of St. Paul's, Sheffield, introduced hymns in his services. The people didn't like it; it wasn't that he chose the wrong tunes, they just didn't like hymns per se. For his efforts, poor Thomas Cotterill was taken to a consistory court. The Chancellor of the Diocese of York ruled that hymns were illegal in Church of England services, but, because the practice had gained a foothold, he didn't feel able to enforce his decision!

This is by way of introduction to the fact that reading today's passage from Mark took me back to a weeklong mission that I was part of in January 1997, in Lithgow, New South Wales. We taught the children to sing a song and, I being unable to resist an opportunity to sing from the pulpit, we're going to give it a go now.

The first line is "Blind man sat by the road and he cried", which repeats twice. What does he cry? In the song, he cries "Show me the truth, Show me the light, Show me the way." In the second verse, we're reminded that Bartimaeus, as well as being blind, was a "Beggar man." In the third verse, it's Jesus who gets to cry: "I am the truth, I am the light, I am the way." Let's give it a go, join in as you get the hang of it.

> Blind man sat by the road and he cried (x3)
> He cried Oh Oh Oh
> Show me the truth
> Show me the light
> Show me the way
> The way to go home baby Ah Ah Ah Ah Ah Ah

Beggar man sat by the road and he cried (x3)
He cried Oh Oh Oh
Show me the truth
Show me the light
Show me the way
The way to go home baby Ah Ah Ah Ah Ah Ah

Let's turn to our passage, which you'll find on p. 981 of the church Bibles, Mk. ch. 10, beginning at v. 46. The passage begins, "Then they came to Jericho." We know from v. 32 that they're on their way up to Jerusalem, and the "they" is "Jesus and his disciples together with a large crowd."

If you're able to make the trip to the Holy Land, you can visit places such as Jericho, which helps identify them as real places. Jericho is reputedly the oldest town on earth. It had been conquered by Joshua 1,400 years before, through the collapse of its walls, recorded in ch. 5 of the Book of Joshua. At the time of Jesus, Jericho was one of the cities designated for priests and Levites to live in; the Jerusalem Temple, where they served, was fifteen miles away. Nowadays, Jericho is a Palestinian town of 15,000 people, situated in what's known as the West Bank, five miles from the Jordan River.

We're introduced to Bartimaeus, the Son of Timaeus, who was blind and a beggar, probably because of his blindness. This is the only time that he gets a mention, his fifteen minutes of fame. Although, of course, he's gone down to history and we find ourselves talking about him now.

Bartimaeus was "sitting by the roadside begging." The disciples were, as we read in v. 32, "on their way up to Jerusalem, with Jesus leading the way." And indeed, the first Christians came to be known as followers of "the Way", Acts 9:2. But, because of his blindness, Bartimaeus was not able to be with them. Instead, he just sat by the roadside, out of the way.

V. 47: "When he heard it was Jesus of Nazareth, he began to shout, 'Jesus, Son of David, have mercy on me!' " Note that it says, "he began to shout." He didn't just cry out once, he continued shouting "Jesus, Son of David, have mercy on me!" He was persistent and insistent, as a desperate man will be. "Jesus, Son of David, have mercy on me!" Hear him crying out repeatedly.

Then we have the self-appointed protection squad for Jesus who, v. 48, "rebuked [Bartimaeus] and told him to be quiet." At v. 13, we read how the disciples had rebuked those who sought to bring little children to Jesus. I think it's the same mentality that had led Peter, James and John to seek to 'save Jesus from himself.' A 'we know best' mentality. When we assume that someone else is "too busy." And it's the mentality of tamed and controlled religion.

Jesus is having none of it. He stops and Bartimaeus hears, "He's calling you", v. 49. What joyous words to hear. To know that Jesus is calling you. Just as Bartimaeus had been persistent in calling out to Jesus, so Jesus doesn't call just once. He continues calling until Bartimaeus is by his side.

Bartimaeus's response is dramatic; v. 50: "Throwing his cloak aside, he jumped to his feet and came to Jesus." If there is joy in hearing Jesus calling you, so too there is joy in responding to his call.

Jesus asks Bartimaeus at v. 51 precisely the same question he had asked James and John at v. 36, "What do you want me to do for you?" This time, what Bartimaeus asks for, "I want to see", is 'for Jesus to grant' and he does so: "Immediately he received his sight", v. 52.

I find Jesus' words, "your faith has healed you", intriguing. In other instances, it's perhaps easier to see how the petitioner's faith has been demonstrated. For example, the faith of the centurion in Mt. 8 and Lk. 7. He tells Jesus, "Lord, I do not deserve to have you come under my roof. But just say the word, and my servant will be healed" [Mt. 8:8]. In saying this, the centurion acknowledges his unworthiness, and his faith in Jesus' power and authority, even to heal at a distance.

Perhaps we need to look again at what it was that Bartimaeus had shouted, that led Jesus to acknowledge his faith: "Jesus, Son of David, have mercy on me!" Bartimaeus had heard that it was "Jesus of Nazareth" who was passing by. This is presumably how others were referring to Jesus. Indeed, it was the conventional and natural way to do so; to identify people by where they came from. But this isn't how Bartimaeus addresses Jesus. Instead, he ascribes to him a Messianic title, the only person to do so in Mark's gospel account: "Jesus, Son of David".

David had been Israel's second and greatest king. At the 'Walk Through the Old Testament' seminar we held last year, he was described as having a 'whole heart' for God. The title "Son of David" was widely used among the Jews to refer to the Messiah. It's derived from Old Testament passages such as Jeremiah 23, vv. 5 and 6: " 'The days are coming,' declares the Lord, 'when I will raise up to David a righteous Branch, a King who will reign wisely and do what is just and right in the land. In his days Judah will be saved and Israel will live in safety. This is the name by which he will be called: The Lord Our Righteousness.' "

By addressing Jesus as "Son of David", Bartimaeus is saying, 'I believe that you are the Messiah, God's anointed one, come to save his people.' As we have just sung, "Hail to the Lord's Anointed, Great David's greater Son!" Perhaps Bartimaeus also had in mind what the prophet Isaiah had said would be a sign of the Messianic age: "Then will the eyes of the blind be opened", Is. 35:5.

Though Bartimaeus could not see, he had great spiritual insight. In using the phrase "Son of David," he revealed his personal knowledge of Jesus' true identity. Clearly, he knew that the Scriptures taught that the Messiah would come from the tribe of David. By calling Jesus the "Son of David," he proclaimed his belief that Jesus was indeed the Messiah of Israel and the Saviour of the world.

Helen Keller was born in Alabama in 1880. At 19 months old, she contracted an illness which left her both deaf and blind. She was once asked, "Isn't it terrible to be blind?" Her response was, "Better to be blind and see with your heart, than to have two good eyes and see nothing." Bartimaeus is an example of someone who was able to 'see with his heart.' Jesus had said to the disciples in ch. 8: "Are your hearts hardened? Do you have eyes but fail to see, and ears but fail to hear?" [vv. 17,18].

I was ordained deacon at St. Philip's Church, Sydney, the one in Australia, you understand, on March 14th 2004, using the 1662 Prayer Book's ordinal. This meant that we also used that Prayer Book's litany, which repeatedly refers to us as being "miserable sinners". This caught the attention of a friend of mine from Canberra who told me: "You Anglicans are very fond of being 'miserable sinners!' " Audrey, being of Northern Ireland stock, was at that time a Presbyterian; I'm happy to say that she has since become an Anglican!

We need to understand what the Prayer Book means by "miserable sinners". It doesn't mean miserable in what's become the conventional sense: gloomily downcast, a misery to be with. It means one who recognises that he's in need of God's mercy. It's a request for forgiveness of sin. Bartimaeus shouted, "Jesus, Son of David, have mercy on me!" Bartimaeus is saying to Jesus, 'I'm in need of forgiveness of sin and I recognise that you can give it.' That's why Jesus says to him, "your faith has healed you."

The Greek word translated "has healed", *sesōken*, also means "has made whole" or "has saved". Bartimaeus has been healed physically; he has also been saved spiritually through his encounter with Jesus. The Prayer Book's catechism describes a sacrament as "an outward and visible sign of an inward and spiritual grace." Miracles, such as the healing of Bartimaeus, also have these qualities. They point beyond themselves to what God is doing spiritually in the life of a person, in this case Bartimaeus.

Bartimaeus had been "sitting by the roadside begging." He was sitting on the side-lines, out of the way. Having been healed by

Jesus, he is now able to "follow him along the road" to Jerusalem. He has become one of Jesus' disciples, his followers.

Bartimaeus has joyously responded to Jesus calling him and, having done so, he now follows him. Jesus is calling us too to follow him. Do you hear his voice calling you? Persistently calling you? And having heard his call, have you responded to it?

In 1852, Cecil Frances Alexander wrote these words:

> Jesus calls us; o'er the tumult
> Of our life's wild, restless sea,
> Day by day his sweet voice soundeth,
> Saying, 'Christian, follow me.'

> Jesus calls us! By thy mercies,
> Saviour, may we hear thy call,
> Give our hearts to thine obedience,
> Serve and love thee best of all.

Amen.

Mark 11:1-11, November 19th, 2017

You may wish to have our passage in front of you; it's on p. 981 of the church Bibles, Mk. ch. 11.

A reminder of what we're about with our current, slightly curious, sermon mini-series: I'm plugging the gaps in our long series on Mark, left from the Sundays when I didn't preach earlier, so I will have preached right the way through his Gospel account. Conveniently, there's only one passage after today, so clearing the decks nicely for Advent; and the promise of a bound volume to come!

The NIV Bible gives today's passage a heading: The Triumphal Entry. It's an event I'll bet my bottom dollar makes most of you think of Palm Sunday. That said, Mark would be mightily surprised to hear that: he knew nothing of liturgical calendars, and would have nothing to say about associating part of his account with a particular Sunday in the year. What's more, the Book of Common Prayer doesn't set this reading for the Sunday before Easter Day.

I can make a case for Jesus' triumphal entry into Jerusalem being a fitting subject for the 'Sunday next before, next before Advent', as a sort of limbering up exercise! There is a move afoot to extend Advent from four to seven Sundays before Christmas Day; not the sort of thing I'm usually into, but with Advent 4 falling on December 24th this year, maybe just this once.

I went to theological college, Hogwarts for clergy. It was a not always agreeable experience: there was a lot of talk of being stretched and broadened; at times it felt like being in the grip of an over-enthusiastic masseur! But at the end of three years, our group had pretty much got the measure of each other.

In one class, we were asked: if you could have just one Gospel account, which would you choose? James, predictably, went for Mark, the oldest and shortest. Karl, equally predictably, countered that by saying Matthew: you get Mark plus added value!

Actually, Mark's and Matthew's accounts of the Triumphal Entry are remarkably similar; Matthew just slips in a couple of Old Testament references. And the Prayer Book sets Matthew's account of the Triumphal Entry for the First Sunday in Advent. Why so?

The connection isn't that difficult to discern; as they say, it's not rocket science. Advent, meaning 'coming to', is about an arrival. One which immediately might spring to mind is Jesus' birth; the Incarnation, which we celebrate at Christmas. That's mentioned in the Advent Collect: "thy Son Jesus Christ came to visit us in great humility". But the Collect also looks forward to "the last day, when he shall come again." When the Bible mentions the Last Day, it's referring to Jesus' Second Coming, something we look forward to.

In the Collect, there's a looking back and a looking forward and a linking of the two. Likewise, our reading from Mk. 11 looks back to a past event; and we're to link it with Jesus' Second Coming. Obviously, both events are to do with Jesus arriving. The interesting bit is that as we delve a little deeper, we discern further linkage.

One of the mysteries we face in the gospel accounts is the several times that Jesus tells people to "tell no one." This is sometimes referred to as the Messianic Secret. Why is it that Jesus should say this? I hope that it feels counterintuitive to you. Do we not have a desire to let people know about Jesus? Isn't this what we are to do? A likely explanation for why Jesus told people not to tell is that the timing wasn't right. He didn't want his earthly ministry to be curtailed early.

But with Jesus' triumphal entry into Jerusalem, the secret's clearly out. The manner in which Jesus entered Jerusalem, with cloaks and branches spread on the road, proclaimed a royal entry. "Blessed is he who comes in the name of the Lord!" [v. 9] is a welcome to the Messiah: Jesus applies it to himself in the following days. Combine it with "Hosanna!", a cry of praise that means 'Save us!', and the people are shouting the equivalent of "God Save the King!" Both of those expressions come from Ps. 118 [vv. 25 and 26], traditionally sung during the Passover festival, which the people are preparing for.

"Blessed is the coming kingdom of our father David!" [v. 10] refers to the promise that God gave King David, that an eternal kingdom would be established ruled by a king in David's line. David had been a great king of the Jews, their greatest king to date. Now here is a king even greater than King David, King Jesus. Praise him for his majesty; and rejoice in his humility, which leads him to the cross to die for our sins.

When Jesus returns at his Second Coming, there will likewise be no doubt about who he is. Paul writes in Phil. 2:10, "that every person will bow down to honour the name of Jesus. Everyone in heaven, on earth, and under the earth will bow" (ERV). Everyone will know about Jesus' coming at that time. It will not be a whole city being stirred as it was when Jesus entered Jerusalem, but the whole world.

Gough Whitlam, Australian Prime Minister during the 1970s, was controversial in many ways. He turned 80 in 1996, the year I moved to Australia. I recall a speech he gave at that time. He was known to be an atheist, but, perhaps moved by advancing years, speculated about what his attitude would be, were he eventually to meet God. With characteristic gravelly drawl, he boasted, "You can be sure of one thing, I shall treat him as an equal." Gough Whitlam died in October 2014. The Second Coming will be a time when "[everyone] will bow down to honour the name of Jesus"; and 'everyone' will include even Gough Whitlam.

The little clause at the start of our passage, "As they approached Jerusalem", marks the end of a long and momentous journey. Jesus, not Pilate, not the Chief Priests, was the true ruler of Jerusalem. Jesus was coming to die in Jerusalem. Jesus would rise from the dead in Jerusalem. Jesus loved Jerusalem; but Jesus was bringing judgement on Jerusalem.

Jerusalem was at the centre of the old Jewish order; and the old order is about to be swept away by Jesus. Jerusalem was under judgement, because Old Testament Israel has proved itself to be unfruitful. It had failed to be what God called it to be. It's about to reject God himself, in the person of his Son, Jesus. When God came to them in Jesus, they killed him.

Thirty years after Jesus there was a Jewish revolt against the rule of the Roman Empire. It was ruthlessly crushed. Jerusalem was laid waste, and the Temple was reduced to rubble. After the death and resurrection of Jesus, it is no longer Jerusalem and the Temple which are the focus of God's presence with his people. It is Jesus himself.

The entry of Jesus into Jerusalem marks a transition to a new era in how God relates to his people. God's people are no longer those who relate to him through the Temple and its sacrifices. They are those who know him through faith in his crucified and risen Son Jesus.

The Book of Common Prayer currently contains this prayer, which I consider to be measured and reasonable:

> O God, who didst choose Israel to be thine inheritance: Look, we beseech thee, upon thine ancient people; open their hearts that they may see and confess the Lord Jesus to be thy Son and their true Messiah, and, believing, they may have life through his Name. Take away all pride and prejudice in us that may hinder their understanding of the Gospel, and hasten the time when all Israel shall be saved; through the merits of the same Jesus Christ our Lord. Amen.

At this year's General Synod of the Anglican Church of Canada, a move to erase this prayer from the Prayer Book failed. The Bishop of Saskatchewan said: "There are many people who would not use this collect, but there are also many who might use it, and for whom the theology of that collect is something that they're comfortable with, and to remove it might seem to say to them that there's no place for that kind of point of view."

I've posted a video by the atheist Penn Jillette, on Holy Trinity's Facebook page; in it he says: "How much do you have to hate somebody to not proselytise? How much do you have to hate somebody to believe that everlasting life is possible and not tell them that?"

Christians, those who "confess the Lord Jesus to be thy Son and their true Messiah", shall inherit and inhabit the "Holy City, the new Jerusalem" depicted in Rev. 21. How much do you have to hate someone, or a group of people, to seek to ban a prayer for them to come to a saving knowledge of God in Jesus?

I'm sorry to say that there's likely to be a renewed attempt to delete the prayer at the next General Synod, to be held here in Vancouver in 2019. My prayer is, "Take away all pride and prejudice in us that may hinder ... understanding of the Gospel, and hasten the time when all Israel shall be saved."

Let's remind ourselves of how the crowds greeted Jesus as he entered Jerusalem: "Those who went ahead and those who followed shouted, 'Hosanna! Blessed is he who comes in the name of the Lord! ... Hosanna in the highest!' "

Crowds are dangerous things. Their mood swings about, sometimes wildly. They can turn on you if you get the wrong side of them. At that time the people wanted to follow Jesus. But what was to happen later that same week? The crowds cried out "Crucify him!" [Mk. 15:13]. They wanted him killed. And he was.

One of the purposes of the Advent season is that we might prepare ourselves. That we might be prepared to celebrate Christmas, when we remember Jesus' birth, 2,000 years ago; but also that we might be prepared for Jesus' Second Coming.

The days are coming, indeed, in all sorts of ways they are already here, when faithful followers of Jesus will have to stand firm against the crowd. Don't fear force; fear God. And don't follow the crowd; follow Jesus. He is just and merciful. He is gentle and powerful. Victory in the end is his. He is the king. Fear no-one else. Follow him.

There were those who cried, "Hosanna!", "Save us!", and those who cried, "Crucify him!" What is your response to Jesus? Are you with those who acknowledge him for who he is, or those who want nothing to do with him? As we enter the season of Advent, may we so prepare ourselves that we too may join in the great cry of "Hosanna!"

Amen.

Mark 11:12–19, July 12th, 2015

We're continuing our journey progressively through Mark's gospel account. Last week, we had Jesus' triumphal entry into Jerusalem. I'm imagining eyebrows being raised at having that passage on July 5th. Surely it's out of context, some might say; it belongs on Palm Sunday. I've said before that I hope that reading progressively through Bible books is helpful to you. I certainly find it helpful for my preaching, because by doing so, we see passages and incidents in their true context, the events with which, in this instance, Mark surrounds them.

As we come to Mk. 11, v. 12 and following, I have in mind things we've looked at in recent weeks. In particular, the arresting passage in ch. 8 when Jesus "rebuked Peter. 'You do not have in mind the things of God, but the things of men' ", Mk. 8:33. And that theme continues: the contrast between God's way, and man's way. Next Sunday we'll look at v. 29 of ch. 11, where Jesus asks the Jewish priests, teachers and elders: "John's baptism — was it from heaven or from men? Tell me!"

That's the true context in which we should be looking at our passage, Mk. 11, vv. 12-19: the stark contrast between God's way, with authority from heaven, and man's way of doing things. Please turn with me to our passage which you'll find on p. 981 of the church Bibles, Mk. ch. 11, beginning at v. 12. The NIV heads it "Jesus clears the Temple"; in older parlance, what we're going to be looking at is called "The Cleansing of the Temple."

First, I want to take us back just one verse. Jesus has entered Jerusalem. On doing so, he headed for the Temple and "looked around at everything". But it's getting late, so he then heads back to Bethany for the night, with the twelve disciples. I mention this to emphasise that what occurs in the Temple the following day wasn't a fit of pique upon suddenly encountering something. Jesus acted quite deliberately. And I think it's helpful for us to have a sense of the flow of Jesus' movements. These were real events that Mark's chronicling, with real people in real places.

The next day finds Jesus and the disciples leaving Bethany and heading back to Jerusalem. We're told by John, ch. 11, v. 18, that Bethany is "less than two miles from Jerusalem". Then Jesus seemingly does a Prince Charles and talks to a fig-tree: "May no one ever eat fruit from you again", v. 14.

We haven't quite gone as far as bringing pot plants to our annual Thanksgiving for Animals and All Creation service. And by pot plants, I mean plants in pots! I know that Gregor Robertson is particularly keen on trees and I count it as a minor victory that I've managed to have the one outside our entrance removed: do please enjoy the view, until the City plants a replacement!

Jesus doesn't have anything against this particular fig-tree or even fig-trees in general. He's just using it as an illustration: it's a metaphor. Indeed, he's willing to see it sacrificed for the sake of his illustration, as we'll see next week.

Fig-trees, along with vineyards, were used by the Old Testament prophets as a symbol of the nation of Israel. For example Hos. 9:10, "When I found Israel, it was like finding grapes in the desert; when I saw your fathers, it was like seeing the early fruit on the fig-tree."

This is what Jesus intended the disciples to understand when they heard him. This was a teaching moment regarding the fate of Israel if it rejects its true king, Jesus. The fact that "it was not the season for figs" backs this up. Had it been the season, then the tree could have been seen to be at fault. But the tree was not at fault; it was the nation that the tree symbolised that was at fault in rejecting Jesus.

With this incident and its concomitant warning ringing in their ears, they reach Jerusalem for a second time and Jesus again entered the Temple area. Then we have an incident which always captured my imagination when I was a child. I tried to reconcile what I'd been taught about "Gentle Jesus meek and mild", so meek and mild indeed, that as a baby "no crying he makes", with people being driven out and tables being overturned. In my mind,

Jesus did it in a very proper and British way — come along now — or perhaps he was Canadian about it and apologised as he did so.

Actually, Jesus was not British, nor was he Canadian. And so I think there was a certain amount of rough and tumble to the incident, as a natural reading would indicate. God may be "slow to anger" but he does get angry when confronted with wrongdoing, a righteous anger. What's referred to as God's wrath.

What was it that was going on at the Temple that could stir Jesus in this way? First there was the fact that ordinary people, seeking to worship God, were being exploited. The people's money, that they had earned, was deemed unacceptable in Temple transactions because it bore Caesar's image. So here was an opportunity to make a profit, fixing the exchange rate between the people's money and that which could be spent at the Temple.

Then, the people were required to present animals for sacrifice to atone, to make up for, their sins. And it wasn't acceptable to bring in animals from elsewhere, they had to be bought on site. A bit like not being allowed to bring your own popcorn into the cinema! And Temple doves weren't cheap. So there was another opportunity to make money on the backs of people's religious observance.

At one level, Jesus was speaking out against people being exploited in the name of religion. He called the religious establishment for what it had become: "a den of robbers", v. 17. But what Jesus was doing also had deeper implications. His actions took place in what was referred to as the Court of the Gentiles. It was an outer court of the Temple, which anyone could enter. After all, they wanted to be able to take money from anyone!

But it became progressively more difficult to proceed into the Temple, depending on who you were. Jewish women could go so far, Jewish men a bit further, approaching the Holy of Holies, where it was held God dwelt. Only the Jewish priests could enter the innermost court, in order to offer sacrifice. Only the High

Priest could enter the Holy of Holies, and even he could do so only once a year, on the Day of Atonement.

When Jesus enters the Temple, he does so not just as a Jewish layman, which is how he's regarded by the Chief Priests and the Teachers of the Law. But what we've already read in Mark shows that he's more than that. As Peter correctly said, "You are the Christ", 8:29. He's one who has power and authority to heal. He's the one at whose transfiguration a voice had come from a cloud: "This is my Son, whom I love. Listen to him!" 9:7.

Jesus enters the Temple as God's Son, not confined to a Holy of Holies, but in the midst of the people, all people. The writer of the Epistle to the Hebrews describes Jesus as being the "great high priest who has gone through the heavens, Jesus the Son of God," Heb. 4:14. Speaking of Jesus' death on the cross, the writer continues: "[Christ] entered the Most Holy Place once for all by his own blood, having obtained eternal redemption", Heb. 9:12.

At the moment of Jesus' death, "The curtain of the temple was torn in two from top to bottom", Mk. 15:38. That was the curtain that gave access to the Holy of Holies. By Jesus' death, God became accessible to all, through faith in who Jesus was and what he had accomplished on the cross. From that moment on, the Temple, with its blood sacrifices of animals, priests on the make, and Holy of Holies, became irrelevant. It was to be destroyed by the Romans in AD 70 and has never been rebuilt.

Jesus had quoted Isaiah, an Old Testament prophet: "My house will be called a house of prayer for all nations." Jesus' clearing the Court of the Gentiles of those who were buying and selling there was symbolic of what he was to achieve through his crucifixion. All nations would be free to come to God in prayer through him.

V. 18: "The chief priests and the teachers of the law heard this and began to look for a way to kill [Jesus], for they feared him, because the whole crowd was amazed at his teaching." It wasn't just that a few tables had been overturned: no doubt they were righted quickly enough after Jesus' departure. It was the implications of what Jesus had done and said that scared the Chief Priests and Teachers of the Law — the implications for their losing their hold over the crowd.

Yesterday, I went on a so-called catacombs tour under the Vancouver Art Gallery. On emerging, I encountered a stall set up by people 'having a go' at religion. I was intrigued by this. One of my thoughts was, how come I've never encountered a stall in Vancouver telling people about Christianity?

I'm afraid that I didn't engage with the people on the stall: I wanted to reuse my bus ticket before it expired! But, looking at their placards, it struck me that they'd weakened their argument by taking a swipe at all religion in general. I think I'd like to have said to them, tell me about the religion you don't like, because I think that it may be something I don't believe in either: the type of religion Jesus encountered at the Temple. Now, let me tell you what it is I do believe.

Amen.

Mark 11:20–33, July 19th, 2015

Please turn with me to our passage, which you'll find on p. 981 of the church Bibles, Mk. ch. 11 beginning at v. 20; the NIV heads it, 'The Withered Fig Tree.' To fully understand Peter's exclamation, we need to refer to vv. 13 and 14. The fig-tree, which the day before had been "in leaf," was now "withered from the roots." And this had occurred as a result of what Jesus had said, "May no one ever eat fruit from you again."

It wasn't that Jesus had anything against fig-trees, either in general or specifically this one. The miracle, Jesus' only destructive miracle, was meant to teach the disciples and us; that's why Jesus had cursed the tree within earshot of the disciples, and fortunately Peter had remembered what he'd said. The chronology of what happened, and Mark's chronicling of it, makes clear its meaning.

In between the tree's being cursed and their seeing it withered, Jesus had confronted what was going on in the Jewish Temple, what's referred to as 'The Cleansing of the Temple', vv. 15–17, with traders being driven out, tables overturned and harsh words for the Temple authorities: "you have made it 'a den of robbers.' "

Fig-trees, along with vineyards, were used by Old Testament prophets as a symbol for the nation of Israel. Israel, exemplified by the Temple, had rejected God and his ways. And now God was to institute a new way of relating to people, all people, through his Son, Jesus. But as well as acting as a teaching-point, what occurred was also a demonstration of Jesus' power and authority, including over nature. The tree had withered just at a word from Jesus.

Our Bible study last Thursday was perhaps even more freewheeling than usual. One of the topics we discussed was a tendency to be overfamiliar with 'my buddy Jesus.' This brought us, somehow, to consideration of the exhortations the Prayer Book provides at Holy Communion, part of which I use at this service. In them we read: "my duty is to exhort you ... to consider the dignity of that holy mystery, and the need of devout preparation for the receiving thereof, so that ye may come holy and clean to such a heavenly Feast, in the marriage-garment required by God in holy Scripture, and be received as worthy partakers of that holy Table." Our discussion also reminded me of a devotional book my mother had been given after her confirmation in 1938, prayers to be said before a Holy Communion service.

Jesus gives us direct access to God, bypassing the sacrificial system the Temple represented. Yes, he is our friend and our brother, human like us: "What a friend we have in Jesus". Yet we should not forget at what price this access was achieved, his sacrificial death on the cross. And he is unlike us in the purity of his humanity, being a sacrifice without sin, and in the fact that he is God.

Some may feel that I'm too stern in this respect and I know that I'm out of step with much of what is preached elsewhere. But having watched an episode of *The Waltons* last week, let me tell you, this is mild compared with Baptist preaching in 1930s Virginia! The 1924 Standard Edition of *Hymns Ancient and Modern* included Henry Chorley's hymn 'God the all terrible'; by the 1950 Revised Edition God had become "omnipotent" instead.

What Henry Chorley had been trying to express was a sense of the power and otherness of God. We find it also in some contemporary songs:

> Be still for the presence of the Lord
> The Holy One is here
> Come bow before Him now
> With reverence and fear
> In Him no sin is found
> We stand on holy ground
> Be still for the presence of the Lord
> The Holy One is here

Or the song 'Only by grace can we enter', which has the chorus "Lord, if you mark our transgressions, Who will stand?" echoing the words of Mal. ch. 3: "the Lord you are seeking will come to his temple [but] Who can stand when he appears?" The song provides the answer: "Thanks to your grace we are cleansed by the blood of the Lamb."

Jesus responds to Peter's exclamation, "The fig-tree you cursed has withered", by telling him to "Have faith in God", v. 22. I see this as further evidence of Jesus' divinity; he was able to do what he did by his word because he is God. Jesus then refers to "this mountain" which would have been the Mount of Olives, just outside Jerusalem, from which the Dead Sea would have been visible.

We're familiar with the phrase 'moving mountains', meaning achieving a seemingly impossible task. It actually predates this incident, as it was a common Jewish idiom. Jesus is using it as a turn of phrase, much as we would. He then teaches about prayer, linking it with belief, drawing upon the fact that Peter has just witnessed God's power to change things in the case of the tree.

Jesus' words in v. 24, "whatever you ask for in prayer, believe that you have received it, and it will be yours", need to be seen in the context of what he says in Jn. 14:14: "You may ask me for anything in my name, and I will do it." That phrase "in my name" is important. To tell someone to "Stop in the name of the king" means you're speaking not on your own authority but that of another, who agrees with what you're doing.

To be effective, prayer requires its alignment with what Jesus would have done. The fig-tree withered because it was Jesus' will that it be so. Faith and belief involve us deepening our relationship with God and aligning our will with his. Jesus himself was to pray to his Father on the Mount of Olives, "not what I will, but what you will", Mk. 14:36. And that should be the basis of all our prayers.

Jesus continues, v. 25, "And when you stand praying, if you hold anything against anyone, forgive him, so that your Father in heaven may forgive you your sins." We're familiar with this from the Lord's Prayer: "Forgive us our trespasses, as we forgive those who trespass against us." We are able to approach God in prayer only on the basis of the forgiveness he extends toward us, and we should be gracious with others just as God is with us. The Prayer Book's exhortations I referred to earlier include: "Ye must also be ready to forgive others that have offended you, as you would have forgiveness of your offences at God's hand." Our prayer is in fellowship with others; as Paul writes in I Cor. 13:2, "if I have a faith that can move mountains, but have not love, I am nothing."

Jesus then enters Jerusalem and goes to the Temple where he is sought out by the Jewish Chief Priests, teachers and elders. They home in on the question of authority; v. 28, " 'By what authority are you doing these things?' they asked, 'And who gave you authority to do this?' " What they really mean is, why aren't you under our authority, doing what we want?

Jesus' reference to John the Baptist reminds me of his parable of the rich man and Lazarus. When the rich man asks Abraham to send Lazarus to warn his brothers, Abraham replies, "They have Moses and the Prophets, let them listen to them", Lk. 16:29. Jesus knows that the Jewish authorities didn't listen to John the Baptist. The implication is that they knew, or should have known, that John's authority was from heaven, but they chose to ignore him. So too, they should be in a position to recognise and acknowledge Jesus' authority. But again, they won't do so.

It's always interesting, I think, to consider where we place ourselves within a story. I think we're being placed by Mark in the shoes of those priests, elders and teachers, in the sense that we need to decide where we stand in regard to Jesus. Just as was the case for them, you've had the evidence laid out before you by Mark; what do you make of it? Do you acknowledge Jesus' heavenly authority?

This is a question which each of us must answer individually for ourselves. But then, it's one we must answer together as a church fellowship. I find it significant that such questions are being asked in the Temple, a place of worship. And Jesus is passing judgement on the Temple because of its failure to acknowledge him and follow him. We too need to think about where the focus of our worship lies. Do we see church first and foremost in terms of worshipping Jesus and acknowledging his authority over us?

Amen.

Mark 12:1-12, July 26th, 2015

Please turn to our passage, Mk. ch. 12, which you'll find on p. 982 of the church Bibles. It begins, "He then began to speak to them in parables." Who is the 'he'? Usually in the gospel accounts, it's reasonable to assume that it's Jesus, and that's the case here. If you have one of the excellent NIV Study Bibles, you'll know it's the case because the dialogue that follows is printed in red. We also know it's the case by looking at the sentence before, at the end of ch. 11.

Who's the 'they'? Again look back to the previous chapter. Jesus is in the Temple in Jerusalem and he's conversing with the Jewish Chief Priests, teachers and elders who work there and who have sought him out.

Things hadn't ended well at the end of ch. 11. You'll see that the NIV Bible has headed vv. 27-33, "The Authority of Jesus Questioned." That's what the priests et al. have been doing, and it's never a good idea. They asked Jesus a question; he responded with another, which they chose not to answer, and Jesus' words to them immediately before our passage were, "Neither will I tell you by what authority I am doing these things."

As you can see, things weren't going well between Jesus and the Jewish leaders. If the scene were being acted out in today's Church, conflict resolution experts would probably be called upon to try to defuse the situation. The Church of England has just set aside half a million pounds to be spent in this way.

But what does Jesus do? He digs the hole deeper. I wonder what you think about the Parable of the Tenants. When Margaret heard that was today's passage she responded, "Good. It's a better story than the one about the fig-tree!" Possibly on hearing it you think, well, it's just a story about a man who owned a vineyard and was in dispute with his tenants, nothing unusual about that: call in the conflict resolution experts!

The Jewish Chief Priests, teachers and elders didn't see it that way. They were fuming! So much so that, v. 12, "they looked for a way to arrest [Jesus] because they knew that he had spoken the parable against them." What had Jesus said that had caused them such offence?

The usual definition of a parable is "an earthly story with a heavenly meaning." This parable has a heavenly meaning: it's about God. But it has an earthly meaning as well. It's about God and his relationship with his people on earth. Jesus is using the parable form, to say things directly against the Jewish leaders. And he's doing it to their face.

There's a man who planted a vineyard. Both vineyards and fig-trees were used by the Old Testament prophets to symbolise Israel. Jesus has already told his disciples, by means of the Withered Fig Tree miracle, that Old Testament Israel was done for, because of the way that they had rejected God. Now he says the same thing to the Jewish leaders, and, in so doing, points the finger at them as the ones responsible.

The Jews, hearing Jesus, would have thought of what the prophet Isaiah had said: "The vineyard of the Lord Almighty is the house of Israel," Is. 5:7. And remember too, the first great gardening project: "the Lord God had planted a garden in the east, in Eden; and there he put the man he had formed", Gen. 2:8. It was clear who the man in Jesus' parable represented: God.

The man provided for his vineyard. "He put a wall around it, dug a winepress and built a watchtower." So too, God provided for Israel's needs. He looked after his people with providential care. And he continues to do so for us. He provides for all our needs. In 1636, Roger Williams founded the capital of Rhode Island and named it Providence, in honour of "God's merciful Providence" in providing for the first American settlers.

Yet the vineyard in the parable was only rented to the farmers. The man retained ownership of it. We do well to remember that that which we have is only entrusted to us to steward for a season.

Everything on earth, everything God has provided, remains his. Ps. 24, v. 1: "The earth is the Lord's, and everything in it, the world, and all who live in it."

In the parable, v. 2: "At harvest time [the man] sent a servant to the tenants to collect from them some of the fruit of the vineyard." This is entirely reasonable, he's collecting the rent. He isn't an unreasonable landlord: he waits until harvest and he's only asking for some of the fruit. But the vineyard's tenants "seized [the man's servant], beat him and sent him away empty handed", v. 3. The man persists in sending servants, but the tenants persisted in their response: "some they beat, others they killed", v. 5.

The man in the parable represents God. The vineyard is Old Testament Israel. Who are the servants? Who are the people God sent to Old Testament Israel as his servants, his messengers? They were prophets: men such as Isaiah. And the response of Israel to the prophets had often been a shameful one, rejecting the message of repentance that they sought to bring from God, just as the servants in the parable were "treated shamefully."

And so, in the parable, we reach the last one that the man had to send, "a son, whom he loved", v. 6. This takes us back to the beginning of Mark's gospel account, to Jesus' baptism. At that time, "a voice came from heaven: 'You are my Son, whom I love' ", ch. 1, v. 11. And also to Jesus' transfiguration, when "a voice came from the cloud: 'This is my Son, whom I love, Listen to him!' " ch. 9, v. 7.

Jesus is identifying himself with the son whom the man sends. He's saying that the man expects his son to be respected. But he's also saying that he knows that this won't be the case. V. 7: "the tenants said to one another, 'This is the heir. Come, let's kill him' ". This echoes the predictions Jesus has given to his disciples about what will happen to him. Ch. 10, v. 33: " 'We are going up to Jerusalem,' he said, 'and the Son of Man will be betrayed to the chief priests and teachers of the law. They will condemn him to death' ".

The reason the tenants give for killing the vineyard owner's son is significant: "the inheritance will be ours." The reason why the man had sent his servants to the vineyard, and latterly his son, was not because he was in need of fruit. It was because he wished to establish a right relationship between him and the tenants: one in which they acknowledged that he was the owner and they were tenants. But all along, it was this that had rankled with them; it was this that they had rebelled against: 'We want to be our own master, rather than mere tenants of yours.'

I recall a parishioner of one of my former parishes, renowned for her feistiness. Over coffee after a service, the conversation went this way: "Remember, this is our church, Karl, not yours!" My response, "Actually, Jean, it doesn't belong to either of us, it's God's." I'm happy to say that, as well as being feisty, Jean was also a great support to me, and I have a beautiful print of Bishop Latimer preaching before Edward VI, that she and her husband Michael gave as a farewell gift.

The mistake that Old Testament Israel kept on making was forgetting their tenant status and the obligation that this placed them under toward God. Time and time again, they thought they knew better and they weren't obedient to him. And now they were to do so again, by rejecting Jesus and killing him.

V. 9: "What then will the owner of the vineyard do? He will come and kill those tenants and give the vineyard to others." The owner had been patient with the tenants, time and time again giving them another chance. The final chance comes when he sends his son, whom he loved. But then comes a time of reckoning and judgement. God has his appointed time for everything, just as "harvest time" was referred to in the parable.

When will the time come when the tenants will be killed? As Jesus leaves the Temple, he says of it, "Not one stone here will be left on another; every one will be thrown down", ch. 13, v. 2. And this came about when the Temple was destroyed by the Romans in AD 70.

Although Jesus and all his first followers were Jewish, the continuing rejection of Jesus as Lord and Saviour by the majority of the Jews was what spurred Paul to turn to the Gentiles, the non-Jews. Acts 18:5: "Paul devoted himself exclusively to preaching, testifying to the Jews that Jesus was the Christ. But when the Jews opposed Paul and became abusive, he shook out his clothes in protest and said to them, 'Your blood be on your own heads! I am clear of my responsibility. From now on I will go the Gentiles.' " By the second century the Church was composed almost entirely of Gentiles: the vineyard that is the Church, the new Israel, had been given to others.

The Jewish Chief Priests, teachers and elders knew what Jesus was saying and they didn't like it; and so "they looked for a way to arrest him." Their reason for not doing so there and then was that "they were afraid of the crowd." This could lead us to think that 'following the crowd' is a good thing. But crowds can be notoriously fickle. Within a week, the Chief Priests were able to stir up the crowd to their way of thinking. And, as a result, we read that, "Wanting to satisfy the crowd, Pilate ... had Jesus flogged, and handed him over to be crucified", ch. 15, v. 15.

The Chief Priests, teachers and elders had questioned Jesus' authority; now they were to reject him. The crowd turned against Jesus as they shouted, "Crucify him!" The Jews at Corinth opposed Paul with his message that Jesus was the Christ, their Messiah. God's truth isn't discerned by finding out what most people think. It's conveyed to us by the messengers that God sends as his servants: the prophets of the Old Testament who point toward the coming of Jesus, at whose transfiguration a voice had come from the cloud saying, "This is my Son, whom I love. Listen to him!"

May we acknowledge that "everything in heaven and on earth is thine O Lord." May we listen to Jesus. The Jesus we find revealed to us through the Bible: the Old and New Testaments. May we not reject Jesus and his teaching, but rather turn to him as our

Lord and Saviour. The Church's one foundation is Jesus Christ her Lord.

Amen.

Mark 12:13–27, November 26th, 2017

This is an historic occasion. In one sense, our series on Mark's gospel account ended on April 3rd last year, when I preached on the latter part of ch. 16. But, as you may be aware, over the last month I've been filling in the gaps left by the Sundays when someone else preached. Mk. 12, vv. 13–27 is the last such gap to be plugged, then I will have done the lot, and the bound volume should shortly be available.

Who was responsible for Jesus' death? Well, there's a thorny issue or can of worms, to mix my metaphors; or is it a hot potato? The Spiritual asks the question, "Were you there when they crucified my Lord?" It seems to imply that the pious answer is yes, and I was 'feeling Jesus' pain.' It can be revealing, when contemplating a scenario, to consider where one places oneself within the narrative.

U2 were perhaps more uncomfortably honest in their song 'When love came to town', which was powerfully performed as part of Pacific Theatre's *Christmas Presence* last year:

> I was there when they crucified my Lord
> I held the scabbard when the soldier drew his sword
> I threw the dice when they pierced his side
> But I've seen love conquer the great divide

The implication of this, is that we're all to blame; and this is true: Jesus died "for the sins of the whole world" and that includes your sin and mine.

Since the Holocaust, Christianity has existed under a cloud of collective handwringing, to mix metaphors again. This has particularly been the case in the academy, but also in the wider Church, particularly higher up the pyramid.

I greatly appreciated going to the Oberammergau Passion Play for the first time in 2010. It's been held in Bavaria, Germany pretty much every ten years since 1634, and I'd love to be part of a group going to the 2020 performance. Since 1990, the Mt. 27:25 reference, "His blood is upon us and also upon our children's children", has been omitted. The same school of thought would like to erase the prayer For the Conversion of the Jews from our Prayer Book. By the way, although the western world may have started going awry in the 1960s, I trace the incidence of major contemporary manifestations of this back to about 1990.

We can't avoid the fact that Jesus' death was an historical event; and at least five Jewish groups were intimately involved: the priests and elders, the scribes or Teachers of the Law, the Pharisees, the Herodians, and the Sadducees. In today's passage, representatives of three of those groups make an appearance. You'll find the passage on p. 982 of the church Bibles, Mk. ch. 12.

V. 13: "Later they sent some of the Pharisees and Herodians to Jesus to catch him in his words." If you're alert, you should be asking the question, who are the "they" that are doing the sending? Look back at 11:27 for the answer and, guess what, it's the other two Jewish groups: the priests and elders, and the Teachers of the Law, who stressed ritualistic religion to the neglect of righteousness.

The Pharisees and Herodians represent an unholy alliance. Regarding the Pharisees, my NIV Study Bible says, "most of those who came into conflict with Jesus were hypocritical, envious, rigid and formalistic. According to Pharisaism, God's grace extended only to those who kept his law."

The word Pharisee literally means separatist: the name was given to them by their opponents because of their holier-than-thou haughty attitude. The Pharisees' ideology can be summarised as: 'I don't smoke and chew, and don't go with girls who do.' They represent the idea that if I keep a long enough list of rules, I'll be in good stead with God.

The Pharisees failed to understand the difference between grace and legalism. Jesus condemned their hypocrisy, evidenced by pride in their outward observance of the Law but inward spiritual void, and their arrogant belief that they were more religious than the rest.

The Herodians meanwhile were "Influential Jews who favoured the Herodian dynasty, meaning they were supporters of Rome, from which the Herods received their authority." They weren't necessarily particularly interested in religious matters per se, only in as much as they impacted the Herodian dynasty. Essentially, they were Erastian: the state trumps all else, an outlook antithetical to that of the Pharisees.

The Pharisees hated Rome and would have nothing to do with Roman rule, making them the unlikeliest of bedfellows with the Herodians. By acting together, the Pharisees and Herodians represent the maxim "my enemy's enemy is my friend"; in this case, the common perceived enemy being Jesus. It was an alliance of expediency. How often is this the case in the world, and even, sadly, the Church.

Their joint assault begins with deceptive flattery, v. 14: "Teacher, we know that you are a man of integrity. You aren't swayed by men, because you pay no attention to who they are; but you teach the way of God in accordance with the truth." These are weasel words, dripping with insincerity: 'Let's lead him on, give him enough rope to hang himself.'

Then there's a sudden switch to a punctiliar question: "Is it right to pay taxes to Caesar or not?" To ram it home, the question is unnecessarily repeated: "Should we pay or shouldn't we?" Each time, it's setup for a 'tick the box' answer, with no intended room for nuance.

The thought is, if Jesus says pay the tax, he'll offend the crowd, his reputation will be shot. If he says don't pay, he'll be arrested for rebellion. Gotcha!

When Jesus replies, "Bring me a denarius and let me look at it", he's adding his own element of drama to the scene. You can imagine the fumbling in the robes and a coin being proffered somewhat reluctantly: this wasn't in the Pharisaic-Herodian script.

A denarius was a silver coin, worth a day's wages, bearing the image of Caesar Augustus. V. 17: "Then Jesus said to them, 'Give to Caesar what is Caesar's and to God what is God's.'"

Jesus would have effectively answered their question by just saying, "Give to Caesar what is Caesar's." Touché. It's true that citizens should submit themselves to the governing authorities as those appointed by God, the exception being if the authorities directly oppose God's teaching in Scripture. But Jesus really does hijack the script when he pointedly adds, "[Give] to God what is God's."

The denarius belonged to Caesar because it bore his image and inscription. What is it then that belongs to God and should be paid to him? You and me. Gen. 1:27: "God created man in his own image ... male and female he created them." We are made in God's image. Furthermore, if we are Christian we bear God's inscription: "you are a letter from Christ ... written not with ink but with the Spirit of the living God, not on tablets of stone but on tablets of human hearts", II Cor. 3:3.

If we belong to God, our lives ought to be totally dedicated to him in honour and respect: "Everything in heaven and on earth is yours [Lord]" and that includes our very selves; "All things come from you, and of your own do we give you", I Ch. 29:11,14. Jesus tells us, "[Give] to God what is God's."

Enter the Sadducees, v. 18, "who say there is no resurrection": that's why they were sad, you see! The Sadducees were priests of the Jewish aristocratic class who exerted powerful political and religious influence, the leading families of the day. They not only denied bodily resurrection, but also the existence of angels, and God's sovereignty over human affairs. Sadducees didn't accept all of the Word of God, and what they did accept they modified to suit themselves.

The Sadducees pose a question for Jesus in the form of a variant on seven brides for seven brothers, the variant being, there's only one bride. Personally, if I were brother seven, or even six or five, I'd be suspicious: was this woman's cooking up to much? The Sadducees' objective, v. 23, is to make the resurrection look ridiculous: "At the resurrection whose wife will she be, since the seven were married to her?"

Jesus' reply in v. 24 onwards answers their question, and also addresses aspects of the Sadducees' skewed theology: "you do not know the Scriptures or the power of God", "the power of God" being a reference to God's sovereignty. At the General Resurrection, "the dead will be raised imperishable and we will be changed" [I Cor. 15:52] through the power of God.

V. 25: "When the dead rise ... they will be like the angels in heaven." Jesus is saying, "You know, those beings that you don't believe in, but I do, not least because the Bible does." Of all the aspects of contemporary theology that are out of kilter with the emphasis the Bible gives, I would posit angels as a leading example. The Bible talks a lot about angels, much more than we do.

V. 26: "God said to [Moses], 'I am the God of Abraham, the God of Isaac, and the God of Jacob.' He is not the God of the dead, but of the living." Abraham, Isaac and Jacob had all died by Moses' day, but God clearly refers to them as being still alive, because they will be resurrected. And Jesus chooses to quote from the Pentateuch, the first five books of the Bible, the part the Sadducees were supposed to believe in.

I've skipped over a part of Jesus' teaching that people often appear to ignore. V. 25 again: "When the dead rise, they will neither marry nor be given in marriage". Yes, if both parties in a marriage are Christian, they will spend eternity in each other's presence; but their relationship will be different then from that of a married couple in this life.

The Sadducees really do represent contemporary thought and culture in so many ways: no supernatural intervention, a puny

God at best, little or no Bible, and as for the afterlife, either fluffy clouds or more likely, just being turned into fertiliser. Basically, little or no hope. As a funeral director once incredulously asked me, "Don't you believe in reincarnation?" No I don't, I believe in the resurrection of the dead.

Article IV of the Articles of Religion: "Christ did truly rise again from death, and took again his body, with flesh and bones, and all things appertaining to the perfection of Man's nature." That was true for Jesus and it will be true for us. That is what we are called to believe; that is what Jesus taught; that is where hope is to be found. To not believe in bodily resurrection is to "not know the Scriptures or the power of God".

Every person, Christian or not, will be physically raised at the General Resurrection and will stand before Jesus as judge at his Second Coming. The verdict will depend on whether you have accepted Jesus as your personal Lord and Saviour.

There's been a lot in the news of late touching on the issue of tax evasion. Italians have something of a reputation for having tax evasion as a national pastime. I've detected that Canadians however, and perhaps Vancouverites in particular, are rather keen on rules and regulations, and seeing that others abide by them. How sad if when a person stands before Jesus, all he has to say for himself is, "I paid my taxes."

Jesus calls us to recognise the sovereign rule of God in our lives, his rule as Lord of all. "There is not a square inch in the whole domain of our human existence over which Christ, who is Sovereign over all, does not cry, Mine!" (Abraham Kuyper). We are to repay to God what is his due.

> Were the whole realm of nature mine,
> That were an offering far too small;
> Love so amazing, so divine,
> Demands my soul, my life, my all.

Amen.

Mark 12:28–37, January 24th, 2016

I've just returned from a trip to Texas. If you need evidence that Canada is different from down south, fly into Vancouver from Dallas and it will hit you! One of the differences, I feel, is that things in the US tend to be very black and white, and I'm not referring to race. But I hope that in Canada, we have space for shades of grey. We need that attitude, when considering the Teacher of the Law we meet in our passage. Please turn to it on p. 983 of the church Bibles, Mk. 12, vv. 28–37.

The Teacher of the Law is one of the Jewish scribes. Let's face it, they're usually the bad guys. They're associated with the Pharisees and Herodians, who we know from ch. 3 were plotting "how they might kill Jesus" [3:6].

But this scribe is different; we shouldn't just lump him in with the rest. V. 28: he'd noticed "that Jesus had given them (that is the Sadducees, Pharisees and Herodians) a good answer". The NIV is a good translation: I like it. But it's known, jokingly, as the 'nearly infallible version' for a reason: it doesn't always get it exactly right.

Actually, I feel a bit like my former Bishop, Tom Wright, at this point; he never seemed to trust any translation except his own. All of the other translations I looked at seem to go with "good answer" or "answered well." But I'm going to hang my translation on the New American Standard Bible, which translates the same Greek word in II Cor. 11:4 as "beautifully." The original Greek has this dimension: the scribe saw that Jesus had answered beautifully.

Now, the scribe gets to ask his question: "Of all the commandments, which is the most important?" The Pharisees and Herodians had been seeking to "catch [Jesus] in his words", v. 13. They'd been asking him questions, seeking to trap him. But that isn't the case here.

Jesus answers by quoting Scripture. It's significant to see how often Jesus did this. Jesus believed in the Bible, in its authority. In v. 30, he quotes from Deut. ch. 6: "Love the Lord your God with all your heart and with all your soul and with all your mind and with all your strength."

I know we're well used to hearing this translation. It comes naturally in English to talk of loving with the heart. But I want to link what Jesus says here, with what he said in ch. 7: "What comes out of a man is what makes him 'unclean'. For from within, out of men's hearts, come evil thoughts, sexual immorality, theft, murder, adultery, greed, malice, deceit, lewdness, envy, slander, arrogance and folly. All these evils come from inside and make a man 'unclean' " [Mk. 7:20–23].

It's not so much that we are to love God with our heart, as if our heart is a tool with which we do something, but rather *from* our heart. So my translation would be "Love the Lord your God out of or from all your heart." Idiomatically, we might say, "Love God from the bottom of your heart."

I could have made the point that, as well as believing in the Bible, Jesus also knew it; he could recite it from memory. But actually, that isn't at all surprising with this verse. Every Jew would have known it well. It's known as the Shema Yisrael, from the first two words of the verse that precedes it: "Hear, O Israel". And this verse gives the reason why we are to love God from all our heart: "the Lord our God, the Lord is one."

If you have many gods, as was the case with pagan religions, you dedicated yourself to any one of them at your peril. What if one of the other gods got to hear of it and became jealous? But as the God of whom Jesus speaks says in Is. 45:22, "Turn to me and be saved, all you ends of the earth; for I am God, and there is no other." There's room for only one God in our lives. Beware, lest you make anything else something that you worship. It might even be something apparently good. But it ceases to be so, if it supplants God as the only one you worship.

With the second commandment, Jesus indicates how we show that we love God; V. 31: "Love your neighbour as yourself." John picks up on this theme in his first Epistle: "If anyone says, 'I love God,' yet hates his brother, he is a liar. For anyone who does not love his brother, whom he has seen, cannot love God, whom he has not seen", I Jn. 4:20.

But actually, Jesus is going further than John does. For John is talking about loving fellow Christians. Jesus' commandment is to love our neighbour. I know we sometimes get caught up on this, thinking it refers to those who live next to us. Actually, neighbour is used in contrast to family: we are to love all people, not just those with whom we have blood ties that would naturally dictate affinity. Although there is something to be said for remembering that neighbour also includes those we live closest to; perhaps it's easier to love at a distance, while those we see the most of can sometimes be the most challenging to love.

The man responds by saying that what Jesus has said is, "more important than all burnt offerings and sacrifices", v. 33. This is a dangerous thing for him to say, considering who he was, a scribe, and where they were, in the Temple, the heart of the Jewish sacrificial system.

Now comes what I regard as the most interesting verse of the passage, v. 34. Jesus "saw that he had answered wisely" and yet gives the man what I see as being a less than full commendation: "You are not far from the kingdom of God."

My mother had two responses when she tried a glass of wine. Either, "Quite good," or else, there would be a significant pause followed by, "Quite good." I feel as if Jesus has just said, "Quite good" to the scribe. "Not far", feels like saying, "The bodies were found in the water, not far from the lifeboat." In such a situation, being "not far" away is not much consolation.

What is the scribe missing? What is it that will get him into the lifeboat and allow him to be saved? It's the difference between knowing what we should do, and actually doing it. Do we love

God from the bottom of our heart? Do we love our neighbour as our self? If we're honest, the answer is no. And the scribe would have known this about himself. Which is why the Jewish religion provided burnt offerings and sacrifices, to make up for the way people fail to love God and their neighbour.

It's not enough for the scribe, or anyone else, just to admire Jesus; he must come to the point where he comes to faith in him and worships him. This gets to the heart of who Jesus is. And it's addressed in the final verses of our passage. Jesus quotes from Ps. 110, written by King David; v. 36: "The Lord said to my Lord: 'Sit at my right hand'".

It sounds like a riddle. There are two Lords mentioned. The first "Lord" David mentions is obviously God. But then, who is the second "Lord" and how can he be David's son? The answer lies in Jesus, born of David's line, a son of David. Jesus here identifies himself as the Christ, the longed for Messiah. And by saying he is the one who will sit at his Father's "right hand", he identifies himself as the Son of God.

Jesus is the only one who has fully loved God from the heart and fully loved his neighbour as himself. And, as such, having lived a life as God intends, he was to die a sacrificial death on the cross, so putting an end to the need for burnt offering or other sacrifices. It's not enough just to admire Jesus, you must bow before him and worship him for who he is, God, and what he has done, paying the price on our behalf, for our inability to do what God expects of us in our lives.

We don't know how the scribe's story develops. Does he come to a point where he recognises who Jesus is, and respond by coming to faith in him and worshipping him? But we can know that about our self. Have you responded to who Jesus is, and what he has done, by accepting him as your personal Lord and Saviour? That is the most important question any of us face.

If you have, when you do, Jesus then gets to work in you, gradually changing your heart, enabling you to love God and your neighbour more fully. Effecting a change of heart in us. It's always going to be a work in progress I'm afraid. But you can look out for signs of God at work.

Perhaps you feel drawn to give more generously to the work of God, a sign that God is at work in you. Perhaps you have a growing sense of the excellence of God. And that emboldens you to speak more freely about him. Perhaps you are drawn to see new ways in which you can love your neighbour.

These are signs of faith in God. Not only do we have assurance of salvation through faith in Jesus. He also helps us to live more fully the life he would have us live in him.

Amen.

Mark 12:38–13:2, January 31st, 2016

I found today's passage from Mark personally challenging. I found myself thinking, "Oh dear, does he mean me?" Jesus starts with, "Watch out for the teachers of the law." The Teachers of the Law, or scribes, may be regarded as one of the categories of Jewish clergy. They weren't the priests, most of whom were Sadducees, who offered sacrifices in the Temple. The scribes' rôle was to teach the people the religious law contained in the Pentateuch, the first five books of the Bible.

The scribes came into their own with the cessation of Old Testament prophecy. The book of the prophet Malachi is the last book in the Old Testament. After that comes what's known as the 'intertestamental period' of about 400 years, until the birth of Christ. I hold that the primary way in which prophecy takes place in today's Church is through preaching. And we can regard the scribes in that way: they were teachers of the Bible and preachers.

Can you begin to see why I might be worried? Coming from a Protestant Reformation perspective, I see my rôle not as a Catholic priest. I don't offer sacrifices on the Holy Table: Jesus has already done that, on the cross at Calvary, once and for all. Rather, my rôle is to preach and teach the Bible. And that's what the scribes were doing. Jesus says, "Watch out for them; beware of them."

Just to grind it in, the scribes wore flowing white robes: say no more! They had, v. 39, "the most important seats in the synagogues and places of honour at banquets." A friend of mine was a Rector in the Black Country, which is a distinctive area of the West Midlands of England, not far from where I grew up. He tells of being invited to a function through his rôle as Rector of the parish. He was to say grace and was seated at the head table. He was disconcerted that his place of honour meant having an uncooked pig's head, complete with apple in its mouth, directly in front of him!

Perhaps it's a good thing that clergy are generally no longer treated with the high regard they once were. The latest figures from an Ipsos Mori poll found that trust in clergy in Great Britain has declined from 85% in 1983 to 71% now. A friend tells of travelling on the New York subway wearing his clerical collar. He merely smiled at a child to earn the rebuke from the mother, "Paedophile!" A cleric at Sydney Cathedral in Australia used to take his collar off if walking in the city: "You get accosted by so many strange people." Was I imagining it, or was the waitress a tad wary when I went out for lunch in Deep Cove after last Sunday's service, still wearing the identifying article?

Jesus says of the scribes, v. 40, "Such men will be punished more severely." It's a sentiment echoed in the Prayer Book's ordination service. The bishop says to those who are to be ordained, "And if it shall happen the same Church, or any member thereof, to take any hurt or hindrance by reason of your negligence, ye know the greatness of your fault, and also the horrible punishment that will ensue." It's a sentiment taken up by James in his Epistle, ch. 3, v. 1: "Not many of you should presume to be teachers my brothers, because you know that we who teach will be judged more severely."

Let's move on to the second vignette in our passage. Jesus is still in the Temple. But now he's moved to what was known as 'the court of women'; it's the last stage in the building that women were allowed into and it's the place where "the offerings were put". Jesus "watched the crowd putting their money into the temple treasury", v. 41. We can imagine it as a busy scene; there was a "crowd" and "Many rich people [throwing] in large amounts."

But Jesus' attention is caught by just one person, a "poor widow". Perhaps we're familiar with the story, so this doesn't surprise us. Perhaps we just think, that's what Jesus would do, that's what he's like. But transport yourself to such a scene. Is the "poor widow" the one you'd be likely to notice and comment upon?

Jesus calls his disciples to him and says, v. 43, "I tell you the truth, this poor widow has put more money into the treasury than all the others." Clearly, this wasn't the case, literally speaking. But he goes on to explain, "They gave out of their wealth; but she, out of her poverty, put in everything — all she had to live on."

Again, I'm not sure that Jesus' had sufficient insight into the circumstances of one woman in a crowd to know that what she gave was literally "all she had to live on." But he's making a point, linked to what he said in last week's passage: v. 30, "Love the Lord your God with all your heart and with all your soul and with all your mind and with all your strength." And we might add, "with all your money."

We use words from David's prayer in I Ch. 29, when presenting the collection at our services: "Thine O, Lord, is the greatness, the power, the glory, the splendour, and the majesty; for everything in heaven and on earth is thine. All things come from thee, and of thine own do we give thee." Do we really believe that? That what we give, is only giving back part of what God has given to us?

The final vignette is also challenging to me. I have an interest in architecture; I was chuffed to be able to pick up *The Oxford Dictionary of Architecture* for $4.50 at Regent College recently. I like "magnificent buildings". I'm not one of those evangelicals who regard a church building as merely something to keep the rain off. I have high aspirations for our new worship space as part of the redevelopment.

But I'm also mindful of an encounter during an outing to Ripon Cathedral while I was a student at Durham. One of my friends said to another something along the lines of "What massive stones! What a magnificent building!" To which Claus replied, he happens to be a German Lutheran, "What a shame that more people don't think of what the building's here for. They don't go beyond admiring the building, to worship the God it represents."

The Temple was indeed magnificent. It had been added to and beautified by Herod the Great. Even by our standards, we'd be impressed. But imagine how it was viewed in its day: stones 12 foot by 12 foot. But impressive as it was, it was to come a tumbling down under the Romans in AD 70, after the Jewish rebellion. And with it came the end of the Jewish sacrificial system; there was no longer anywhere to sacrifice.

Incidentally, this is sometimes given as a reason for dating Mark's gospel account after AD 70; he knew about the Temple's destruction and wrote it into the story. I'm not so cynical. I go with the majority view that Mark's was the first gospel account to be written, probably in the 50s or early 60s.

Let's tie our three vignettes together; what is the common theme? It's to do with externals versus the heart of the matter. The scribes were concerned about externals: flowing robes, being greeted, important seats, places of honour, getting rich. Now, not all of the scribes were guilty of these things. We can think about the scribe we looked at last week, the one whom Jesus saw as having answered wisely. But many of them were guilty as charged.

You may have felt that I was a bit hard on the clergy earlier on: I hope you did! The fact is there are many good clergy who fulfil the expectation laid upon them at ordination: "consider how studious ye ought to be in reading and learning the Scriptures and in framing the manners both of yourselves, and of them that specially pertain to you, according to the rule of the same Scriptures." But there are some clergy who are, well, not so good at this.

The scribes' prayers were long, but were they heartfelt? At the ordination, the bishop reminds us that ministry is not just a matter of our own minds and wills: "for that will and ability is given of God alone: therefore ye ought, and have need, to pray earnestly for his holy Spirit." That's why an active, personal prayer life is so important, for all of us, reflecting a personal relationship with God. Do you pray regularly, in your own homes?

The widow with her two copper coins reminds us that, just as it's not externals that matter, so too, this is not just about 'head stuff'. More important is where the heart is. We are to love God with a whole heart; from the bottom of our hearts. Remembering that "where your treasure is, there your heart will be also", Mt. 6:21 and Lk. 12:34. Jesus says of the scribes and Pharisees, "Isaiah was right when he prophesied about you hypocrites; as it is written: 'These people honour me with their lips, but their hearts are far from me' ", Mk. 7:6.

If you take an honest look at your heart, what do you see? Do you see attributes of the scribes bubbling up sometimes? Do you see the sublime surrender of the widow? I would think you're probably like most of us, if we're honest; you see a mixture of both. There will be areas of your life you've given over to God, and other areas you currently keep to yourself.

For myself, my prayer is, Father, shine your light into my heart. Expose the parts that are still like the scribes: impressed by external things, power structures, fleeting beauty, intellect, status. Show me where these things lie, that I may surrender them to you. Father, show me where I desire adulation more than seeing you honoured; where I'm more interested in my praise than yours.

Father, forgive; and he does and he will. For the sake of Christ who lived the life that we fail to; a life of sublime surrender to his Father's will. Father, for his sake, forgive me and give me the heart of the widow: a bold, trusting, undivided heart.

Amen.

Mark 13, February 7th, 2016

I hope there's value for you in our practice of sequential reading and preaching through Mark's gospel account. Cast your mind back, if you will, to ch. 11, Jesus' triumphal entry into Jerusalem. In the Church's liturgical calendar, we mark that on Palm Sunday, the Sunday before Easter. Everything that occurs in chs. 11–15 fits into one week, Holy Week, with the final chapter, 16, dedicated to the Resurrection on that first Easter Day.

It's the same in all the gospel accounts, even more so in John: a disproportionate amount of space is dedicated to the Passion narrative. If you need evidence that Jesus was the man born to die, here it is. You're missing the point if you just see Jesus as a good or wise man whose life and example we are to emulate. For the whole purpose of his life is summed up in this last week. Something we can't emulate, only marvel at.

Please turn to our passage, Mk. ch. 13, which you'll find on p. 984 of the church Bibles. For the last couple of chapters, Jesus has been in and out of the Temple. Now, at the beginning of today's passage, he leaves it for the final time. And, we find him, v. 3, "sitting on the Mount of Olives", where he was to pray in the Garden of Gethsemane on the night of his arrest, "opposite the temple". Do you see the symbolism?

Jesus then tells Peter, James, John and Andrew about two events: one to occur in what, for them, was to be the relatively near future, the other in the more distant future. These events are intertwined in the narrative, in such a way that it can be difficult, but not impossible, to untangle them. The two events are: the destruction of the Temple, which occurred in AD 70; and Jesus' return and the end of the earth as we know it, which has yet to occur.

It's appropriate that these two occurrences should be bracketed together because there's a relationship between their significance. The destruction of the Temple marked an end of Judaism as it had existed to that moment. There could be no more sacrifices, because there was nowhere to sacrifice. And an end of the concept of God having a fixed abode: there was no Temple for him to abide in. Along with the Temple, Jerusalem was destroyed as a city and the Jews were scattered, the Jewish diaspora.

This marked, in many ways, the end of civilisation and religion as it had existed, certainly as far as the Jews were concerned. It was the end of their world as they had known it. And the same can be said about what will occur at Jesus' return.

You can find all sorts of weird and wonderful things via the internet. Something I came across was the question of how long it would take for any trace that we'd been here to disappear if mankind were to be suddenly wiped out. The bottom line was that it wouldn't take long, relatively speaking. Nature would take over, and even our proudest monuments would crumble without a trace.

That's not what the Bible says will happen; that's not the way Jesus says things will occur. But, at his return, we'll have to get used to a totally new way for things to be. John in Rev. 21, talking about those times, says, "Then I saw a new heaven and a new earth, for the first heaven and the first earth had passed away".

I have high hopes for the new Holy Trinity building that will result from our redevelopment project. But it will become redundant at Jesus' return; it will 'pass away'. We'll have to get used to a new way of worshipping in God's immediate presence. No more Holy Communion services, remembering, looking back; imagine that!

I indicated that it is possible to get a sense of when Jesus is referring more directly to the destruction of the Temple, and when he's talking more directly about his return. The clue is to look for when he says, "these things", referring to the destruction of the Temple; and when he says, "those days", referring to his return. Thus, v. 30, "I tell you the truth, this generation will certainly not pass away until these things have happened", is talking about the destruction of the Temple, within the disciples' lifetime; whereas "those days" in v. 24 is referring to his return.

Regarding his return, Jesus says, v. 32, "No one knows about that day or hour, not even the angels in heaven, nor the Son, but only the Father." Jesus says even he doesn't know; but that doesn't stop people from speculating! There's quite an industry out there, busily interpreting passages such as ours, and saying, this bit fits with this, now must be the time, or just around the corner. But in fact "no one knows".

When I was in Boston, immediately before coming to Vancouver in January 2014, I visited the John F. Kennedy Presidential Library on its outskirts. It chronicled the Cuban Missile Crisis of 1962. This is my excuse for quoting what I think is one of the best lines from the black comedy film *The Butcher Boy*, based on the novel by Patrick McCabe. It's set in rural Ireland. Some women are listening to an account of the crisis on the radio, to which one of them says, "It'll be a bitter day for this town if the world comes to an end"!

Or what about the so-called Millennium Bug, remember that? Actually, a computer friend of mine let on that this was just a scam by those in the computer industry to generate lots of work for themselves updating computers!

It's part of the arrogance of each age that it likes to think of itself as special. The fact is, we've been in the 'last days' or 'end times' for the past 2,000 years. There's nothing to mark our age as special in this respect. Take one of the signs, "wars and rumours of wars," v. 7; name a time when the world hasn't been at war somewhere.

Jesus refers to these signs as being "the beginning of the birth pains", v. 8. Paul writes, "We know that the whole creation has been groaning as in the pains of childbirth right up to the present time", Rom. 8:22. That describes the Christian's state throughout time, as we await Jesus' return and "wait eagerly for our adoption as sons, the redemption of our bodies" [Rom. 8:23].

The irony about those in the 'end times' predictions industry is that they're doing what Jesus says we shouldn't do, and, as a result, not doing what he says we should. There's what I find a delightfully helpful image in v. 34: Jesus says, "It's like a man going away: He leaves his house and puts his servants in charge, each with his assigned task."

The Reformer John Calvin emphasised that each of us as Christians has our own calling and associated tasks to fulfil as part of God's plan and purposes. Jesus' call to us is to do the things we should be doing as Christians: 'staying awake and watching' involves us praying, and putting God first in all that we are and do.

Having said that, I want to comment on two of the signs. V. 5: "Jesus said to them: 'Watch out that no one deceives you. Many will come in my name, claiming, 'I am he,' and will deceive many.' " Two things are worrying about this. First, the deceivers will come in Jesus' name. They will present themselves as Christian leaders. Second, there will be many of them, and many will be deceived.

This can actually be a source of solace if you find yourself taking a minority stance: it doesn't mean that you're necessarily wrong. I worry about the American Episcopal Church's theology, which appears to equate the work of the Holy Spirit with votes in its General Convention. As Article XXI of the Thirty-nine Articles of Religion states, regarding General Councils, "when they be gathered together, (forasmuch as they be an assembly of men, whereof all be not governed with the Spirit and Word of God,) they may err, and sometimes have erred, even in things pertaining to God." And this can apply to Diocesan Synod, the Anglican Church of Canada's General Synod, even to Parish Councils!

How are we to discern between truth and falsehood then? The deceivers point to themselves, "I am he." A truly prophetic voice takes a stance akin to that of John the Baptist, pointing not to himself but to Jesus. And a truly prophetic voice takes what Jesus says in v. 31 seriously, "Heaven and earth will pass away, but my words will never pass away." We must allow ourselves to be bound and constrained by the words of Scripture.

The other sign I want to comment on gives a good counterbalance to the deceivers. V. 10, "the gospel must first be preached to all nations." This is something regarding which considerable progress has been made over the past 150 years. And even more so over the last 50 years. Yesterday, I sat next to a Filipino whose remote village was evangelised by American Episcopalians — they get some things right! — after the Second World War; the village is now 100% Anglican. This should be an imperative to us in our evangelism efforts; effective proclamation of the gospel is part of staying awake and watching.

In 1971 Paul McCartney had a hit with the song 'Another Day':

> Every Day She Takes A Morning Bath she Wets Her Hair,
> Wraps A Towel Around Her
> As She's Heading For The Bedroom Chair,
> It's Just Another Day.
>
> Slipping Into Stockings,
> Stepping Into Shoes,
> Dipping In The Pocket Of Her Raincoat.
> Ah, It's Just Another Day.
>
> At The Office Where The Papers Grow She Takes A Break,
> Drinks Another Coffee
> And She Finds It Hard To Stay Awake,
> It's Just Another Day

On the day of Jesus' return, people will be expecting "Just another day." But it won't be just another day; it will be the last day. V. 26, "At that time people will see the Son of Man coming in clouds with great power and glory." It will not be an event that can be missed or mistaken. It will have more in common with Jesus' triumphal entry to Jerusalem when "the whole city was stirred" [Mt. 21:10], than with his comparatively low-key birth.

That fact, along with the imperative to preach the gospel to all nations, speaks loudly against the privatisation of belief that is prevalent in our culture. I can't resist making reference to just one more sign of the 'end times'. V. 9: "You must be on your guard. You will be handed over to the local councils". I know this comes from the fallen side of my nature, but I'm rather hoping I'll be near someone from the City's Planning Department at Jesus' return; so I can point out, "This is why the Church is important!"

The destruction of Jerusalem in AD 70 was disastrous for those who put their faith in that city. But God replaced the concept of the Old Testament nation-state of Israel, with the concept of a New Israel, that encompasses the whole earth and is composed of all people who acknowledge Jesus as their personal Lord and Saviour. The hymn 'Come ye thankful people come' expresses this concept: "All the world is God's own field / Fruit unto his praise to yield."

What Jesus prophesied regarding Jerusalem came true. So too, we can put our trust in what Jesus says about what will happen at his return. The way to prepare for this is first and foremost by turning to him and accepting him as your personal Lord and Saviour. Have you done this? Don't leave it too late, as many will do. All will have to bow before him at his return; how much better to be doing so as those he has redeemed, than as those he has not.

As Christians, we are to stay awake and watch. This involves allowing ourselves to be bound and constrained by Scripture. Being regular in personal Bible study. Abiding by Jesus' words that "will never pass away." Responding to God's call upon our lives, in all he calls us to do as part of his plan and purpose. Being people of prayer, and putting God first in all we do and are. And being faithful in our witnessing of Jesus' saving power to others, that the gospel be preached to all nations. At Jesus' return, may he find us to be such a people and such a Church.

Amen.

Mark 14:1-11, February 14th, 2016

I have recently watched two recently-made biblical epic movies: *Noah* and *Exodus: Gods and Kings*. I liked them. But in doing so, I appear to be, as ever, out of step with many people. I guess the general attitude of non-Christians toward these movies is indifference; why bother? And many Christians have moaned, because the storyline and script don't follow the Bible verbatim. I feel as if I want to say to those Christians: lighten up!

I know there are evangelicals for whom any artistic interpretation of the Bible is anathema. I'm not one of them. I think our world would be a sadder place without music and visual art. And, for me, the pinnacle of both of these is when they seek to express what it is to be Christian, to know God through Christ. God gives us gifts and talents which should be used to his glory. And his glory is not diminished by the intervention of artistic interpretation, even artistic licence.

I actually prefer *Exodus: Gods and Kings* over Cecil B. DeMille's 1956 version, *The Ten Commandments*. Why so? Perhaps I find the earlier film's earnestness a little cloying. But in addition the most recent adaptations help me see the characters as real people, caught up in real events. There's an earthiness and grittiness about the depiction of life in ancient times, which I think is helpful and more accurate.

The Bible can be regarded as just words on a page. Or it becomes something to be dissected; and this can be a failing of both liberal higher criticism, and of the use of the Bible as a source of doctrine removed from reality. But at its most powerful, the Bible is story. The story of God's interaction with his people through Jesus Christ.

We're currently hearing Mark's telling of that story. Our passage contrasts two characters: Mary and Judas. Please turn to your Bibles at p. 985, Mk. ch. 14. The scene is set in the first couple of verses. The Passover is "only two days away". For those of us who know how the story will end, we know we're almost there. It's Tuesday of Holy Week: two days before the Last Supper; three days before Jesus' crucifixion.

"The chief priests and teachers of the law were looking for some sly way to arrest Jesus and kill him." Actually, there's nothing new in this. We were told in ch. 11 of their beginning to look for a way to kill Jesus. And back in ch. 3, the Pharisees and Herodians had banded together with the same intent. They had a motive to kill Jesus — he was a threat — now Judas was to provide them with the means and opportunity to do so.

V. 10; "Judas Iscariot [was] one of the Twelve." He had been selected by Jesus to be part of his inner circle. He had spent three years with Jesus. Imagine the insights he could have gained. He could have gone down in history as one of the Apostles on whose ministry the Church is built. Instead, he was to blow it; his place taken by Matthias; Judas' fate was ignominy. And for what? Mark gives a heavy hint: "they promised to give him money", the love of which is "a root of all kinds of evil", I Tim. 6:10.

A source of sadness is knowing of people who were once, apparently, strong Christians, who subsequently abandon their belief. I remember talk when I was a student at Durham, of people who had been leading members of the Christian Union, but who had subsequently fallen away. People who'd had the advantage of knowing the gospel, but had then rejected it, having allowed themselves to be ensnared by other concerns. Perhaps worse are those who remain in Christian ministry, despite no longer believing what they once did.

The actions of the Chief Priests, Teachers of the Law and Judas are contrasted with those of the woman who, v. 3, "poured [expensive] perfume on [Jesus'] head." We know from John's description of this incident, in ch. 12 of his gospel account, that the woman was Mary, the sister of Martha and Lazarus. John also identifies Judas as being among those who criticised Mary's actions.

Vv. 4 and 5 of our text: "Some of those present were saying indignantly to one another, 'Why this waste of perfume? It could have been sold for more than a year's wages and the money given to the poor.' And they rebuked her harshly."

Jesus makes it very clear where he stands on the matter. He, in turn, rebukes those who had been rebuking Mary. V. 6: "Leave her alone ... She has done a beautiful thing to me." I know whose sandals I'd rather be in at that moment! Imagine how Mary's self-esteem would have been raised, hearing those words: "She has done a beautiful thing to me."

Did Judas' inability to take criticism add to his motive for then wanting to betray Jesus? Maybe. Although John gives another reason for Judas' rebuke of Mary: "He did not say this because he cared about the poor but because he was a thief; as keeper of the money bag, he used to help himself to what was put into it", Jn. 12:6.

My experience is that there's a difference in the way that contemporary Christianity is expressed. There are those who emphasise what is sometimes referred to as the social gospel. This has at its core justice issues; righting what are perceived as social wrongs. There's no doubt that the plight of the poor lies close to Jesus' heart: "Blessed are you who are poor, for yours is the kingdom of God", Lk. 6:20. But Jesus makes it clear what must lie at the heart of the Church's message. V. 7: "The poor you will always have with you, and you can help them any time you want. But you will not always have me."

This points to Jesus' impending death, and its centrality in any message the Church proclaims. We don't have Jesus with us in the way he was present at Simon's table. But he is present with us nonetheless, through his Spirit. As Jesus points out, we can help the poor any time we want. Amongst us, we have ample resources to do so. But our incentive for doing so is what we believe about Jesus, and our desire to share that message.

Michael Curry was elected Presiding Bishop of the Episcopal Church last year. One of the things that has been said about him is that he speaks a lot about Jesus. Apparently, this marks him as distinct from his predecessors. And I've also heard it said that Fred Hiltz, Primate of the Anglican Church of Canada, has also started talking more about Jesus, perhaps taking his cue from Michael Curry. God moves in a mysterious way His wonders to perform!

As Christians, we must talk the Jesus talk, as well as walking the Jesus walk. A converted heart, having accepted Jesus as your personal Lord and Saviour, having a personal relationship with God through Jesus, who he is and what he has done for you, is an essential starting-point. As is a willingness to articulate this to others.

I heard of this advice being given to clergy: pray and do what you can. It's an antidote to the malaise where, if we're conscientious, we never feel we're doing or achieving enough. The key is prayer. If we're in tune with God's will through prayer, he will show us what we should, and should not, be doing, and give us the means to carry this out. It's a similar sentiment to that expressed by St. Augustine: "Love God and do whatever you please: for the soul trained in love to God will do nothing to offend the One who is Beloved."

Jesus says of Mary, v. 8, "She did what she could." Oh to be in Mary's sandals once more! Imagine hearing Jesus saying, 'Karl did what he could.' That is all Jesus asks of us, that we do what we can, what he calls us to, what he enables us to, no more and no less.

In our passage, Mark places Mary's actions in stark contrast with those of Judas. Mary is motivated by extravagant love for Jesus, hang the expense. Judas appears to have been motivated by a love of money and concomitant love of self.

I don't believe that either Mary or Judas realised the full significance of what they were doing at the time. Mary didn't think of her pouring perfume as preparation for Jesus' burial; she needed

Jesus' interpretation to know that. Judas' remorse, recorded in Mt. 27, indicates that at the time he didn't realise where his actions would lead.

But Mary's action was right and she was praised for it; whereas Judas' action was wrong, whichever way you look at it. And so Mary goes down in history as among the righteous, whereas Judas stands condemned.

Jesus doesn't call us necessarily to do great things for him. It can be arrogance to presume that you are the one who is going to change the world; it's up to God to do that. But Jesus does call us to be faithful. Perhaps in little things. The things he calls us to do; the things he enables us to do; the things we know we can do and should do, that are right because they are what Jesus would have us do.

How blessed to hear Jesus say of oneself, "She has done a beautiful thing for me; he did what he could; well done, good and faithful servant."

Amen.

Mark 14:12–26, February 21st, 2016

I mentioned when we looked at ch. 13 of Mark how all the action of chs. 11-15 takes place in one week, which we now know as Holy Week, the week in which Jesus was to die. Mark has set a cracking pace in telling his story up to ch. 10. There've been lots of 'immediatelys', as we seemingly race through three years of Jesus' life and ministry. But now, the pace slows right down. Ch. 14 is the longest in Mark's gospel account, 72 verses. Mark is saying to us: this is the important part, we've reached the crux of the matter.

Please turn to ch. 14, which you'll find on p. 985 of the church Bibles. Last Sunday, we looked at the beginning of the chapter. Jesus was in Bethany, a village about two miles from Jerusalem. It was Tuesday: "the Passover and the Feast of Unleavened Bread were ... two days away" [14:1]. Today, we pick up at v. 12, and it's Thursday, "the first day of the Feast of Unleavened Bread." Curiously, none of the gospel accounts say anything about what happened on the day in between; we don't know anything about the Wednesday.

Mark sets the scene for us in vv. 12-16. The scene is being set literally, as it's about finding the room in Jerusalem where they will be for the meal. But Mark is also providing us with clues about the significance of what is to occur. He does so by means of repetition. I wonder if you spotted it? The term "prepare" is used three times and the term "Passover" is used four times. This, I think, is significant.

We heard the account of the first Passover in our reading from Ex. 12. The Israelites were slaves in Egypt. The Passover was the means by which they were to leave and settle in the Promised Land. It was a nation-building moment. They were to "observe this ceremony" [Ex. 12:25] afterwards, and they did so every year, for 1,200 years. In doing so, they looked back: the ceremonial meal derived its significance from what had happened back in Egypt.

Mark is saying to us that the 1,200 year Passover tradition is preparation for our understanding of what is about to occur, in that upper room in Jerusalem, as Jesus gathers with his disciples.

It's mere coincidence that we're looking at this passage on the one Sunday a month when we don't have Holy Communion: I didn't plan it that way. But I'm going to take advantage of the fact that today's service is Morning Prayer, to say something you may find surprising. Today's passage isn't about Holy Communion. Or, to put what I want to say another way, if we jump straight from the Last Supper to Holy Communion, we'd be making a mistake.

We derive what we are familiar with as our service of Holy Communion more directly from Paul's account in I Cor. 11. There, it had become an observance of the early Church. And we continue that tradition they had established. But that's not what Mark is doing in his account of the Last Supper. To reinforce this he, along with Matthew in his account, omits any reference to the words, "do this in remembrance of me."

So, what is the Last Supper about? It, along with the time spent in prayer in the Garden of Gethsemane that follows, is preparing Jesus and his disciples for Jesus' death that is to occur the next day. Jesus hands his disciples two staple foods, bread and wine: bear in mind that in days before safe drinking water, wine, heavily watered, would have been drunk in the way that we're used to being presented with water when we first sit down at a table in a restaurant.

Jesus' doesn't consecrate the bread and wine. He merely gives thanks, much the way that we would say grace before a meal. As he hands them bread and wine, he says, "this is my body", "this is my blood." Obviously, the bread and wine weren't literally his body and blood. His body was before them; his blood was still coursing through this veins. But the bread and wine represented his body that was to be hung on a cross, and his blood that was to be shed.

There's much discussion about who was to blame for Jesus' death. Was it the Jews? Was it the Romans? In our passage, Jesus points his finger at the disciples. V. 18, "I tell you the truth, one of you will betray me — one who is eating with me." And in doing so, he points the finger at us.

We'll be singing the Spiritual 'Were you there?' in four weeks' time on Palm Sunday: it's in the RHB (1971), no. 460. Were you there when they crucified my Lord? Were you there when they nailed him to the tree? Were you there when they pierced him in the side? Sometimes it causes me to tremble, tremble, tremble: were you there when they crucified my Lord?

In a sense we, as Jesus' disciples, were there and are there. We're there in our culpability, which we share with the Twelve. It wasn't just Judas; they all betrayed Jesus. V. 50: "Then everyone deserted him and fled." We each betray Jesus, every time we chose something or someone as more important than him. Jesus' suffering is caused by those of us who follow him.

I mentioned that Mark intends us to see the Last Supper in the light of the Passover tradition. At the first Passover, a lamb was killed, providing the means of deliverance for the Israelites. At the Passover meal, lamb was eaten in remembrance of that deliverance. Jesus is the lamb who was to be crucified the next day, providing deliverance for his followers. Eating bread and drinking wine at the Last Supper replaces eating lamb.

Jesus says to his disciples, regarding the bread, "Take it" [v. 22]. They are being offered something: a participation in the benefits of his death in terms of the deliverance it offers. But, in order to receive, they must be willing to hold out their hands and take. There is symbolism in the fact that we take the bread and cup at Holy Communion, as the Prayer Book stipulates, into our hands, and so receive.

We receive the benefits of Jesus' death through faith. Not faith in Holy Communion. Not faith in bread and wine. But faith in

Jesus. That he died for you. We are not called to be eucharistically-focussed; we are called to be Christ-centred. When Jesus says in Jn. 6:53, "I tell you the truth, unless you eat of the flesh of the Son of Man and drink of his blood, you have no life in you", he isn't referring to Holy Communion. He means believing that he was to die for you. And that's a faith we can embrace and share right now today, at this service of Morning Prayer.

We read at v. 24 Jesus' words as translated by the NIV: "This is my blood of the covenant, which is poured out for many." I think that the variant reading, which is provided as a footnote, is more accurate, ask me afterwards if you want to know why: "This is my blood of the new covenant."

The Passover meal was an ordinance of the Old Covenant or Testament: both words translate the same Greek word, meaning a witnessed agreement. The Last Supper signifies the New Covenant or Testament, that is about to be instituted by Jesus through his death.

The Old Covenant was made with the Israelites and marked the establishment of them as a nation. The New Covenant is more generous and gracious in its scope. It isn't restricted to a nation in the sense that the Old Covenant was restricted to Old Testament Israel. Rather it is "for many", which means for all who are willing to receive Jesus as their personal Lord and Saviour. If you have done so, you are part of the New Israel, a family of faith in Jesus that is the Christian Church, that extends around the whole world.

The newness of the covenant Jesus institutes through his death is emphasised in v. 25, when he says, "I tell you the truth, I will not drink again of the fruit of the vine until that day when I drink it anew in the kingdom of God." The kingdom of God is both a present reality and a future hope. It was inaugurated through Jesus' death and resurrection, the start of something new. It will achieve its consummation at his return, when he will say from his throne, "Behold, I am making all things new" [Rev. 21:5, ESV, NAS].

Amen.

Mark 14:27–52, February 28th, 2016

I hope that you're finding our week by week progression through Mark as helpful as I am. What we're getting through Lent is an extended look at Holy Week, the last week of Jesus' life. Last Sunday was the Last Supper, in the upper room in Jerusalem. At the end of last week's passage, we read that they sang a hymn and then went out. Out from the security of the upper room, out of the city, into the open, to the Mount of Olives.

I've seen people who wear WWJD bracelets: 'What Would Jesus Do?' I've never been tempted to wear one myself. Partly because, well, wearing things like that just isn't my thing. But if it was, I think there are more legitimate messages to wear. Such as, WDJD 'What Did Jesus Do?'; or WWJ 'Who Was Jesus?'. If you really want a message that relates to your actions, then I think the legitimate question to ask is WWJHMD 'What Would Jesus Have Me Do?'

The fact is, Jesus is unique. We can't replicate his life in ours. The uniqueness of Jesus is illustrated in today's passage: in Jesus' interactions with the disciples, with his Father, and with those who come to arrest him. Please turn with me to our passage, which you'll find on p. 985, Mk. ch. 14, beginning at v. 27.

Who was Jesus? He was his Father's Son. He says as much twice. First, in v. 36, when he addresses God in prayer as "Abba, Father", the use of the intimate Aramaic term indicating the closeness of his relationship with God as his Father. Then, in v. 41, in his use of the term "Son of Man" of himself. This is equivalent to Jesus calling himself the Son of God.

"Son of Man" is a Messianic title. In the Old Testament, Daniel had this vision about the Messiah: "there before me was one like a son of man, coming with the clouds of heaven. He approached the Ancient of Days and was led into his presence. He was given authority, glory and sovereign power; all nations and peoples of every language worshiped him. His dominion is an everlasting dominion that will not pass away, and his kingdom is one that will never be destroyed", Dan. 7:13,14. A similar vision of Jesus as the Son of Man is recorded by John in ch. 1 of the Book of Revelation, as he looks forward to the end of time.

During Lent, we have Morning Prayer on Tuesdays, Wednesdays and Fridays. Knowing that I wouldn't be around last Wednesday — I was at a preaching seminar at diocesan HQ — I arranged for Sharon to lead Morning Prayer. She prepared for it, and turned up, only to be told by at least one person that she, Sharon, was "far too busy" for such an activity! Friends, none of us is ever too busy for prayer. It is when I am at my busiest, that I most need to pray. Part of Jesus' essential preparation for what lay before him was prayer.

On September 20th last, we sang this hymn by James Montgomery (it's no. 449 in the BHB (1938):

> Lord, teach us how to pray aright,
> with reverence and with fear;
> though dust and ashes in thy sight,
> we may, we must draw near.

Prayer is something in which we can emulate Jesus. Indeed, Jesus takes "Peter, James and John along with him" when he prays, v. 33. It is true that Jesus eventually says, "It is enough!", a more correct translation of v. 41, meaning 'I have prayed enough'. Even Jesus didn't spend all his time in prayer; there was also a time for action. I struggle with the concept of monastics who seclude themselves from the world in the name of prayer.

It is right that we should share Jesus' prayer to God the Father, "not what I will, but what you will", v. 36, a sentiment included in the Lord's Prayer, "Thy will be done." What we lack is the absolute determination of God's will, and the absolute ability to align ourselves with it. That is what Jesus had, and only Jesus can have, born of his intimate relationship with God his Father.

We should also emulate Jesus in another respect. It's perhaps surprising, considering who Jesus was, God's Son, and the intimacy and immediacy of the relationship he had with his Father. But despite this, Jesus still places himself under the authority of Scripture, and acts in conformity with it. Twice in our passage, Jesus refers to Scripture as charting the path that must be followed: v. 27, "for it is written: 'I will strike the shepherd, and the sheep will be scattered' ", a quotation from Zechariah; and v. 49, "the Scriptures must be fulfilled."

How do the disciples fare? They've been with Jesus for three years. They've just participated in the Last Supper. They have a shocking wakeup call as Jesus tells them, v. 27, "You will all fall away." Peter leads the disciples' chorus of disavowal of this: v. 31, "Peter insisted emphatically, 'Even if I have to die with you, I will never disown you.' And all the others said the same."

But what happens? They fall asleep. V. 37, "Could you not keep watch for one hour?" Then they meet the violence of those coming to arrest Jesus, with violence: v. 47, "one of those standing near drew his sword". The final verdict on those who had insisted emphatically that they would never disown Jesus comes in v. 50: "Then everyone deserted [Jesus] and fled."

Except it's not the final verdict. That, in a sense, came back in v. 28. Even knowing that the disciples "will all fall away," which they do, hear what Jesus says to them beforehand: "after I have risen, I will go ahead of you into Galilee." Can you hear the graciousness in those words? Jesus knows what the disciples are like; he knows what they will do. Yet they remain his disciples, and, after his resurrection, he will be there to lead them.

Are we better than those disciples? I don't think so. We might like to add our voice to that chorus of "I will never disown you", yet we're continually wont to do so. Inside us, there's the little child, caught with his hand in the jam jar, jam smeared all over his face, yet still saying, "I didn't do it."

Part of my fascination with the apocalyptic genre in film and TV drama is seeing how people react in extremis, when the veneer of civilisation is stripped away. It often isn't pretty. Yet even knowing this about us, Jesus doesn't disown us. Instead, he's there for us: "I will go ahead of you." "Saviour, like a shepherd lead us, much we need thy tender care."

The message of our passage is that we must let Jesus be Jesus and do what he must do, and only he can do. Peter said that he would die with Jesus. But he doesn't. And it's right that he didn't. Because only Jesus could die the death that he did: a sacrificial death on our behalf.

Jesus did this voluntarily, as God the Son, in obedience to his Father's will. Everything points to this. The fact that Jesus leaves the security of the upper room; he doesn't cower behind a locked door. Rather he says, v. 42, "Rise! Let us go!" Not escaping from danger, but walking steadfastly toward it. Submitting to those who come to arrest him. And Jesus did this as a dutiful response to Scripture: "the Scriptures must be fulfilled."

I've heard the cross reinterpreted as a tragic accident. As merely an example of man's inhumanity to man. Doing so misses the point, and is frankly arrogant because it puts the ball back in our court, taking the spotlight off Jesus. Jesus did what he did, in obedience to his Father, in fulfilment of Scripture, and for our sakes. The sinless one died in our stead, that sin and death might no longer have dominion over us. Our primary attitude, in response to this, should be one of gratitude.

Jesus didn't call upon us to take up his cross but rather our cross. We must accept that only Jesus could die the death he did because of who he is, and he did it for us. What would Jesus have me do? Follow him, the risen Lord Jesus, knowing that, despite my failings, he will be there to lead the way.

Amen.

Mark 14:53–72, March 6th, 2016

Today, in our following of Mark's depiction of the events that led up to Jesus' crucifixion, our passage homes in on two characters: Jesus and Peter. It may not be immediately apparent, but there's good news to be found for us in both of these. It's my task today to help you see it.

Please turn to p. 986 in the church Bibles, Mk. ch. 14, beginning at v. 53. Jesus is brought before an impressive line-up: "the high priest, and all the chief priests, elders and teachers of the law." It's remarkable that in an age of many wandering preacher-teachers Jesus should command such attention. Clearly he'd made an impact, for all of Israel's brightest and best to band together to see what could be done.

What sort of trial was this? Even by the standards of the time, it was unusual, if not to say illegal. Consider the hour. We know it was late from the fact that, while Jesus had been praying in the garden of Gethsemane, the disciples had kept falling asleep. What sort of court meets in the middle of the night?

What about its location? No doubt the high priest, Caiaphas, lived amidst suitably plush surroundings, even impressive in their way. But what sort of court meets in a person's home, rather than in a courtroom?

And what of the court's purpose? We might presume that a court is there to determine guilt or innocence, but we're told in v. 55, that the judge and jury, "the chief priests and the whole Sanhedrin were looking for evidence against Jesus so that they could put him to death."

It comes as no surprise that this was their sole interest. Back in ch. 11, v. 18, we were told that, "The chief priests and teachers of the law heard this and began looking for a way to kill [Jesus], for they feared him." And in the first verse of ch. 14 we read that, "the chief priests and the teachers of the law were looking for some sly way to arrest Jesus and kill him."

This was a kangaroo court, constituted with one intent: to deliver to those who composed it what they wanted, Jesus' death, come what may. Even so, they struggled. "Many testified against him," v. 56, but apparently they hadn't got together to coordinate their lies sufficiently, and so "their statements did not agree."

Some said, v. 58, "We heard him say, 'I will destroy this man-made temple' ", which wasn't an accurate report of what Jesus had said: "Destroy this temple, and I will raise it again in three days", Jn. 2:19. And so, we're told that again, "their testimony did not agree", v. 59.

Then the high priest intervenes. Things weren't going well as far as he was concerned. He asks the question, v. 60, "What is this testimony that these men are bringing against you?" What indeed. We could answer that, as he should have been able to: it was false and contradictory.

But then a direct question: "Are you the Christ, the Son of the Blessed One?" The high priest is asking Jesus, "Are you the Messiah we've been waiting for? Are you the Son of God?"

Jesus response is equally direct, v. 62, "I am". His uttering of those two words together had significance in themselves, echoing Ex. 3:14: "God said to Moses, 'I am who I am. This is what you are to say to the Israelites: I am has sent me to you.' " Jesus fleshes out his answer by quoting from Dan. 7:13. There was no doubt about what he was saying: what you have asked about me is the case; it is true.

This really was the crux of the matter. If the court had any real purpose, it was to determine whether what Jesus was saying about himself was the case or not. If it wasn't, then yes, he deserved to die, for it was blasphemy. But what if it was true?

The irony was that the entire Jewish religious system was focussed on waiting expectantly for the long promised Messiah. But the Jewish leaders, duly assembled, couldn't bring themselves to countenance that Jesus might be he.

Perhaps Jesus offended their sensibilities: a carpenter, from Nazareth, the Messiah? But perhaps any Messiah would have received a less than warm welcome from them, despite what in theory was the case. For he would turn their world upside down. They had vested interests in keeping things as they were, thank you very much.

No, they weren't interested in investigating the truth of Jesus' claim about himself. Instead, we see them in their true colours. The high and mighty, duly assembled? The great and the good of Israel? More like a band of thugs. V. 65: "some began to spit at him; they blindfolded him, [and] struck him with their fists".

Let's turn our attention to Peter. Where was he while all this was going on? What was he doing? Back at v. 54, we were told that "Peter followed [Jesus] at a distance, right into the courtyard of the high priest. There he sat with the guards and warmed himself at the fire." That detail is repeated at v. 67: "Peter [was] warming himself".

We're not told, but I've no reason to think that Jesus was seated whilst being interrogated and then assaulted. But Peter? Well, he was seated and he was warming himself.

Peter starts off following Jesus "at a distance". This takes him as far as the courtyard. But things start getting too hot, so to speak, when one of the servant-girls starts challenging him. Then, v. 68, he retreats further, "out into the entryway."

Peter's observable concerns are his own comfort and his own safety. He wants to fit in, to not be noticed. Unfortunately, his accent gives him away. V. 70, "Surely you are one of them, for you are a Galilean."

Perhaps at this Peter goes into panic mode. What he then utters is his lowest point ever. We read at v. 71, "He began to call down curses on himself". The word 'himself' isn't in the original Greek; it just says, 'he began to curse.' I can't think why Peter would curse himself; I'm afraid that I find it more likely that he cursed Jesus: "I don't know this man you're talking about."

Luke's telling of the parable of the Good Samaritan ends with Jesus asking "Which of these do you think was a neighbour to the man who fell into the hands of robbers?" [Lk. 10:36]. The expert in the Law can't bring himself to articulate the obvious answer: the Samaritan. Instead, he refers obliquely to "The one who had mercy on him" [Lk. 10:37]. Likewise, at this point, Peter can't even bring himself to say Jesus' name: "I don't know this man you're talking about."

I said at the start that I'd endeavour to bring you good news from today's passage. I'll admit that what I've presented so far doesn't appear that way. Seen individually, both Jesus' and Peter's are sorry tales. But I believe that Mark presents them side by side for a purpose.

How do we know what occurred? It's highly likely that Mark got his account first-hand from Peter. I can imagine Peter saying to Mark: tell it how it was, 'warts and all'. People need to know this; people need to know this about me. Why so?

When you hear an account, where do you imagine yourself in the story? Peter intends us to see ourselves in his place. He's imagining Christians who follow Jesus, but only at a distance. He's thinking of those he knows, whose first concern is their own comfort, rather than Jesus: sitting, warming themselves by the fire. He knows our tendency to want to fit in with those who surround us; not to standout for Jesus, preferring to retreat "out into the entryway." Peter says to you and me: such was I, but I changed, and you can change too.

We're also in the same position that the high priest was when he heard Jesus make that claim about himself: "I am". I am the Christ, the Messiah, the Son of God, the second person of the Trinity: I am God. Is this a claim that you're willing to take seriously enough to investigate it? Is it true? Or are you like so many, who've already made their mind up about Jesus, either without looking at the evidence for his claims, or else in spite of the evidence?

I can see why people do this, for if it is true, it's life-changing. It'll turn your life upside down. That's what following Jesus closely does to you. You'll stand out. You have to put Jesus first, rather than thinking of your own security and comfort. Are you prepared to do so?

Jesus said, "Destroy this temple, and I will raise it again in three days." The temple to which he was referring was his own body. It was 'destroyed' by those who sat in judgement over him, when they nailed him to the cross the next day. But three days later, he rose again, on that first Easter Day.

The Sanhedrin sat in judgement over Jesus. But when he quoted from the Book of Daniel, Jesus spoke of a time when he will return, as judge of all. When Peter "broke down and wept", at the end of our passage, that was the start of his path to redemption. They were tears of repentance: for what he had said, for what he had done.

We need to come to that point when we acknowledge our need of Jesus: for who he is, for what he has done for us. For his willingness to suffer and die on our behalf; in our place. That is the good news: that Jesus was willing to go through with what he did, for people just like Peter; people like me and you.

Amen.

Mark 15:1–20, March 13th, 2016

There is an inconvenient truth at the heart of Christianity: Christianity is based on the suffering and death of a man. I attended a preaching workshop led by Jason Byassee of VST. You may recall when Jason preached here in January. The workshop was about preaching in Lent. Jason touched on the unpopularity of preaching on the cross. I remarked at the workshop that it was 'inconvenient' that Jesus died on a Friday. This, combined with the fact that, in celebration of the Resurrection, we conventionally meet on a Sunday, adds to the temptation to bypass the cross.

I recall a church in Birmingham, my home city, where parents called for a large crucifix to be removed from outside: it scared their children. Really? Or was it nearer the truth to admit that it offended them to be reminded of death, and specifically the death of Jesus.

If we take the gospel accounts at their word, as God's Word, they don't help with our inbuilt desire to avoid the facts of the cross. Rather, they devote much space to the events of the week that led up to it: the Passion narrative.

When I come to prepare a sermon, I find myself asking the exegetical question: what did the inspired writer, in this case Mark, intend me to take away and present to a congregation? When it's narrative, as in today's passage, there's also the question: where do we place ourselves within the account? With whom do I chose to identify?

I suspect that were I to ask you that question, you might be drawn to give what sounds like a pious answer: with Jesus; I'm there alongside my Lord, feeling and sharing his pain. The hymn 'O valiant hearts' seems to encourage this, with its reference to "our lesser Calvaries." I noticed that Microsoft Word's spellchecker doesn't like the word 'Calvaries', and nor do I.

From time to time, British newspapers carry stories of clergy who incur the wrath of the British Legion, by not allowing 'O valiant hearts' to be sung at Remembrance Day services. I avoided that fate, by just dropping the 'lesser Calvaries' verse. Jesus' sacrificial death at Calvary is unique.

As we heard two weeks ago, Jesus' disciples didn't so much fall away from him, they ran. Remember Peter: "I don't know this man" [Mk. 14:71]. Are we so different?

Please turn to our passage, Mk. ch. 15, which you'll find on p. 987 of the church Bibles. Mark mentions three groups of people: the Chief Priests, the crowd, the soldiers; plus one other individual, Pilate. He mentions them not just because they were there, but for a purpose. I want us to look at each, and discern what Mark is saying to us through them.

It's very early on that first Good Friday morning, the day on which Jesus was to die. I'd add to the tortures that Jesus is going through, sleep deprivation. He hadn't slept when the disciples did at Gethsemane; and he'd been interrogated through the night. Now we read that "the chief priests, with the elders, the teachers of the law and the whole Sanhedrin, reached a decision." What was that?

A decision they'd reached long before was that Jesus had to be killed, to be done away with. But how? They didn't have the power to exact the death penalty; they had to rely on Pilate for that.

We know why they wanted Jesus out of the way: it was because of his claim to be the Christ, the Messiah, the Son of God, which they weren't willing to countenance. But such a reason would cut no ice with Pilate; he wouldn't give them what they wanted on that basis. For that, Jesus had to be presented as an insurrectionist. Hence he's bound, as if representing a physical danger.

We know what the Chief Priests' accusation was, from Pilate's question of Jesus in v. 2, "Are you the king of the Jews?" In the Greek original, Jesus' response is just two words: "You say". Our translation fills it out a bit: "Yes, it is as you say." Idiomatically,

Jesus is saying yes to Pilate's question, but he's also saying, 'I'm more than just king of the Jews, as you imagine that.' As John's account tells us, Jesus adds "My kingdom is not of this world" [Jn. 18:36]. Jesus' heavenly kingship means he is king of all.

Pilate, as v. 10 tells us, sees through the Chief Priests' schemes. He knows, v. 14, that Jesus has committed no crime. He knows what he should do: release Jesus. But he's too weak to do so. So he passes the buck to the crowd, and then panders to them.

The crowd, so easily "stirred up", as, v. 11, the Chief Priests are able to do. So easily swayed. The joy of being able to shout loudly, without having to take individual responsibility. They get what they want: "A murderer they save / The Prince of life they slay." They demand the life-taker, Barabbas; they reject the life-giver, Jesus.

Then the soldiers: they have no thought for who Jesus is, why he's there; he's just a convenient target for their mockery. How often this is the case now: people who've chosen not to consider Jesus seriously, but feel free to mock him, to take his name in vain. I note that the media are far more tolerant of poking fun at Christianity than at any other religion.

There you have it: one man, Jesus, standing for truth against so many. There are the Jewish religious leaders. They lie; poorly as it happens, for Pilate sees through them. They are meant to stand for truth in the name of God. But they prefer religion their way, with no room for Jesus and the truth he represents.

We can see this in religion and religious leaders now: either in bigoted fundamentalism, advocating holy war; or else in platitudinous, anything goes religion that fails to lead people to Jesus as the way, the truth and the life.

There's Pilate; poor, pathetic Pilate. Yes, it's tough at the top; with power comes responsibility. It's just not good enough to duck responsibility, and we shouldn't let Pilate off the hook. Pilate knew what the right thing to do was, but he fails to do it.

How often are we let down by those in positions of leadership who choose to settle for the easy life! For whom collaboration means that that which should be done doesn't have to be. How many people, in their heart of hearts, know the truth about Jesus, as Pilate did, but fail to act on it!

There's the crowd. How convenient, even comforting to be part of the crowd! Your name is never going to be called out for posterity's consideration. The crowd is a gang writ large. Everyman. The crowd will always choose someone most like themselves; and so they chose Barabbas, the real insurrectionist, and rejected Jesus. Perhaps they shared a motive with Judas. Jesus had disappointed them as a leader against the Romans. Look at him standing there: bruised, bloody, covered in spit.

What was Mark's intention in giving us details about the parts the Chief Priests, Pilate, the crowd and the soldiers played? Was it just to give a detailed account, and for no other purpose? I don't think so; there's plenty of other detail he could have provided but doesn't.

Partly, what Mark tells us is so we can't conveniently point a finger and say someone in particular was to blame; they were all in it together. But there's also the question of where we place ourselves. Each of these groups, and what they represent, says something about us.

The times we've held to a Christless religion, one more to our own liking, made in our own image rather than his. The times when we should have led, but failed to do so. When we knew what was true, but failed to act upon it. When we've preferred to be part of the crowd, rather than speak out against it. The times when we have mocked Jesus, or failed to speak out when others mock him.

Three times in our passage it says that Jesus was "handed over". Ostensibly this was by the Chief Priests and by Pilate. But Peter, in Acts 2:23, says of Jesus, "This man was handed over to you by

God's deliberate plan and foreknowledge; and you, with the help of wicked men, put him to death by nailing him to the cross."

Jesus' death was not just a random, preventable injustice. He could have called upon angels to save himself at any point. Instead, "steadfast he to suffering goes, that he his foes from thence might free." Jesus had to suffer alone, just as only he could die the sacrificial death that was the purpose of his life. A death on our behalf.

Jesus died for us. Yet, to receive the benefit of his death, we have to admit our part in what drove him to it. It's just not good enough to see ourselves alongside Jesus, and see his suffering and death as being caused by others. We must see ourselves in our true colours, as we really are. It is only then that we are able to see how marvellous what Jesus has done for us is, and embrace it for ourselves, just as he embraces us.

Amen.

Mark 15:21–47, March 20th, 2016

Please turn to our passage, which you'll find on p. 987 of the church Bibles, Mk. ch. 15, beginning at v. 21. We've reached the climax of Mark's gospel account. This is what the preceding chapters have been leading up to. There have been constant intimations that Jesus is to die, and that his death is the focus of his life and ministry. Yet there's an irony for the preacher. The events of this passage are so significant that it's difficult to know what to say about them.

Mark's telling is taut; epitomised by the sentence that begins v. 24: "And they crucified him." Somehow, you don't want to add to what Mark wrote: it feels it is enough. As Paul says in I Cor. 2, "When I came to you, I did not come with eloquence or human wisdom as I proclaimed to you the testimony about God. For I resolved to know nothing while I was with you except Jesus Christ and him crucified."

Tom Wright, also known as N.T. Wright, was my bishop when I was a curate in Durham Diocese. I remember moaning to him about the church where I was on the staff: "I don't recall it ever being explained why Jesus died." "What, not even on Good Friday?" he asked. But Good Friday, in spite of being, in some ways, the obvious time to explain this, just doesn't feel right as a time of explanations. Somehow, you just want to sit with the events.

Today is our Good Friday come early. I can see why some might prefer to preach on Jesus' triumphal entry, and then skip straight to the Resurrection next Sunday. But our reading through Mark, which began two years ago, has been designed to culminate with the crucifixion this Sunday, followed by the Resurrection on Easter Day. There'll be opportunity for you to dwell individually during Friday's Matthew Passion service; but for now, I want to draw out some aspects of Mark's account.

Richard Dawkins is sometimes referred to as the 'high priest of atheism'. But I was struck by an occasion when he was introduced using some such words. In response, he said that he'd never claimed to be an atheist, rather an agnostic. This clearly threw his introducer, so Dawkins went on to explain that he was only 90% certain there wasn't a God. This came as a revelation to me. Would I want to be in the shoes of someone who was only 90% certain about something so important? What about the other 10%? What if it were true?

At his crucifixion, Jesus appeared to be surrounded by people who were only 90% certain about what they were doing. The Chief Priests and Teachers of the Law, who had orchestrated his death, say in v. 32, "Let this Christ, this King of Israel, come down now from the cross, that we may see and believe." And at v. 36, a man who offers Jesus wine vinegar to drink says, "Let's see if Elijah comes to take him down."

They remind me of a university friend, with whom I had conversations about Christianity. He, likewise, wanted 'a sign'. Some sort of writing in the sky. But I am reminded of Jesus' words in Lk. 16, "If they do not listen to Moses and the Prophets, they will not be convinced even if someone rises from the dead." [Lk. 16:31].

Jesus could have come down from the cross, but he chose not to. His attitude was all along that expressed to his Father at Gethsemane: "not what I will, but what you will" [Mk. 14:36]. Had Elijah intervened, it would have been to say, 'I know that you can come down of your own accord, but you mustn't, for my sake and that of others. If you do, then we are lost.'

Sometimes we dwell on Jesus' physical suffering, which was real enough. He even chose not to take the myrrh offered to him as a sedative in v. 23. But the real depth of his suffering is expressed in his words in v. 34, known as the cry of dereliction: "*Eloi, Eloi, lama sabachthani?* ... My God, my God, why have you forsaken me?"

This was an expression of what it cost for Jesus to take away my sin. At that moment, he was separated from God the Father. To feel abandoned by God would be devastating for any of us. But for Jesus, given the intimate nature of his relationship with his Father, it must have been more so. That cry was an expression of what it meant for him to carry the burden of God's wrath in our place. Our forgiveness came at such a price.

V. 37: "With a loud cry, Jesus breathed his last." John tells us that the cry consisted of Jesus saying, "It is finished" [Jn. 19:30]. In one sense, an expression that his life was over, his pain and suffering ended; but also having the sense of 'It is accomplished', that which he came to do. Through his death, Jesus accomplished our salvation, paying the price for our sin: 'It is accomplished.'

As an expression of this, at that moment, v. 38, "The curtain of the temple was torn in two from top to bottom." The curtain separated off the Holy of Holies, the place where God dwelt. No-one was able to have access, apart from the high priest once a year — and then only through the shedding of sacrificial blood. Now, through Jesus' death, we have direct access to God, accorded by Jesus' sacrificial death, once for all.

I shy away from entering into an explanation of penal substitutionary atonement theory, which I believe, at a moment such as this, since somehow it just doesn't feel right to do so. It is like being present at a deathbed or a graveside. Just being there is enough and you don't want too many words. But I will share Stuart Townend's poetry about this moment, from his song 'How deep the Father's love for us':

> Behold the Man upon a cross,
> My sin upon His shoulders
> Ashamed I hear my mocking voice,
> Call out among the scoffers
>
> It was my sin that held Him there
> Until it was accomplished
> His dying breath has brought me life
> I know that it is finished

I've mentioned the Chief Priests and Teachers of the Law, and the man who offered Jesus wine vinegar. But there were others present, whose attitude was different. Among them, Simon of Cyrene. It's significant that Mark mentions that Simon was "the father of Alexander and Rufus" [v. 21]. From this we may deduce that they were known to Mark and to those for whom he was initially writing. Perhaps Simon was already a follower of Jesus. Or perhaps, through this encounter, he became one.

And the centurion, v. 39, most likely in charge of overseeing the execution. We're told that when he "heard [Jesus'] cry and saw how he died" he broke with his code of professional conduct to say, "Surely this man was the Son of God." He didn't keep with what those around him were saying about Jesus, but rather expressed what he believed, based on what he had experienced.

I wonder where you find yourself. Perhaps you are a follower of Jesus, having already accepted the salvation he offers through belief that he died for your sins; you believe that "by his wounds we are healed" [Is. 53:5]. If so, may this recounting of Jesus' death be a reassurance of sins forgiven and salvation assured. Perhaps this is an opportunity to thank Jesus for what he has done for you, through his willingness to die on the cross on your behalf.

But perhaps you find yourself at the foot of the cross for the first time. You may be someone new to church. Or you may have been coming for a long time. But it's now that it strikes home to you what Jesus' death means for you personally. The fact that although he could have come down from the cross, he chose not to do so. And he made that decision, in obedience to his Father's will, on your behalf.

If you find yourself in that situation, now is the time to say to God that you're sorry for your sin that caused Jesus to die. But also that you're grateful, and willing to accept his free gift of salvation, through believing that Jesus is the Son of God, and that his death has paid the price in full of your sin.

Let us pray. Lord we stand before the cross, with a broken spirit. Through the cross, speak to our hearts that word of pardon and acceptance, so that we may be gripped by your love in Jesus Christ and brimful of thanksgiving. May we now go out into the world to live our lives in his service. In Jesus' name we pray.

Amen.

Mark 16:1–8, Easter Day (March 27th) 2016

On Saturday evening, three women did their shopping. They bought spices. A dear friend had died the day before and they wanted to show their respects. They got up early the next day: it was Sunday, the first day of the week. They knew where they were going: to the tomb of their dead friend. They knew what they would do there: anoint his body with the spices. They were well organised and well prepared. Except that, on the way, a thought struck them: what about the large stone that blocked the entrance? Nevertheless they continued.

On reaching the tomb, they saw that the stoned "had been rolled away." That was unexpected, but it wasn't a particular cause for alarm. In fact, it was rather convenient: it solved a problem for them. And so they went in. Inside, "they saw a young man dressed in a white robe sitting on the right side, and they were alarmed" [v. 5]. Were they alarmed just because they hadn't expected to find another person there; after all, it was still very early? Did they feel uncomfortable being alone with a man they didn't know? Was there something about him that was alarming?

Matthew tells us that the "young man" was, in fact, an angel. Perhaps the women detected that there was something special, different, about the young man. I'd imagine that an encounter with an angel, a supernatural being, particularly in a setting like a graveyard, might well be alarming. Remember the reaction of the shepherds, when an angel appeared to them in the fields near Bethlehem: "they were terrified" [Lk. 2:9]; so much so, that the angel had to tell them, "Don't be afraid" [Lk. 2:10] -- this angel tells the women, "Do not be alarmed".

The angel continues: "You are looking for Jesus the Nazarene, who was crucified." If I were one of the women, I might be thinking, tell me something I don't know! Yes, we're here for Jesus' body, and we've got our spices ready. And thank you for reminding us that he was crucified, something of which we're all too painfully aware. At least the angel confirmed they were in the right tomb!

But there is significance in the words the angel uses. He accurately describes the state in which the women had come. They came for the body of a man, their friend, Jesus the Nazarene. That was what they were expecting to find, not unreasonably as they'd witnessed him being crucified. They knew he had died; they knew his body had been placed in this tomb. So, where was it?

Then the young man says seven words that turn their world upside down: "He has risen! He is not here." Their heads would have been spinning. What did he say? Did you hear what I did? What does he mean?

Perhaps he perceives their confusion. And so he continues in as practical and clear a way as he can: "See the place where they laid him." Presumably, they do as he says. And they see ... nothing; certainly not a body.

I was genuinely shocked to read last week about the Revd. Gretta Vosper, a United Church minister in Toronto. Perhaps I was more shocked at the things I read about the United Church. I learnt about something called the New Curriculum: "a provocative educational text produced by the United Church that emphasised the importance of moral teachings over doctrinal beliefs, and challenged Christians to question whether parts of the Bible were historically true."

The newspaper article stated: "There has been a slow but growing movement in the United Church toward downplaying Jesus and the Bible, and moving toward a more metaphorical interpretation of religious symbols and a greater emphasis on humanist, environmental and social justice causes."

Vosper was quoted as saying, "The teaching in theological colleges ... doesn't lead prospective ministers toward a literal interpretation of the ordination questions ... very often, when people come out of the process of discovery, they no longer hold those as literal concepts."

Professor Kevin Flatt, who has written a book about the United Church, said, "My sense is there are a lot of ministers who ... don't really believe in anything resembling traditional Christianity." And Vosper's punch line was, "Clergy who don't believe are a dime a dozen."

This offends me, because it makes me wonder whether people reading the article might think of me in this way, a sort of guilt by association. Whatever the shortcomings of the theological college I attended as part of preparation for ordination, I was never encouraged to think that the Bible wasn't true. When I answered the questions put to me at ordination, I didn't have my fingers crossed behind my back.

But actually, the greater offence is toward those women at the tomb: "Mary Magdalene, Mary the mother of James, and Salome". What are those like Vosper saying about them? Were the women deluded, believing what they wanted to be the case, in spite of the evidence? But their account makes it clear that they fully expected to find a body. The absence of a corpse scuppered their plans: they'd even shelled out good money on spices, to no effect. Or are we to believe they were lying?

I say what I say, in defence of the honour and reputation of the women who were actually there. I put my money on the witness of their first-hand experience, ahead of the views of anyone else. For me, it has the ring of truth. And this is the stance of the Anglican Church. Article IV of the Thirty-nine Articles of Religion states: "Christ did truly rise again from death, and took again his body, with flesh and bones, and all things appertaining to the perfection of Man's nature."

The Chief Priests and the Teachers of the Law had said, "Let this Christ, this King of Israel, come down from the cross, that we may believe" [Mk. 15:32]. The centurion who "heard [Jesus'] cry and saw how he died" said, "Surely this man was the Son of God!"

[Mk. 15:39]. The centurion saw and believed. His witness and that of "Mary Magdalene, Mary the mother of James, and Salome" is good enough for me; I too believe.

A close friend of yours dies. You attend the burial. Three days later, you go to pay your respects at the grave, taking some flowers with you. On arrival, you find the grave open; but you'd seen the digger fill it in three days before. You look into the grave. The coffin's there, but with the lid off, and it's empty apart from the shroud. There's no body to be seen. How would you feel? I think my emotions would be bewilderment mixed with anger. Who has done this?

The women at the tomb were at an advantage in two respects compared with the scenario I've just depicted. The young man was present to provide an explanation, albeit a challenging one, that still left them "Trembling and bewildered" [v. 8]. But it would have begun to chime in with things that Jesus had said: "he must be killed and after three days rise again", Mk. 8:31; "They will kill him, and after three days he will rise", Mk. 9:31.

The women still "fled from the tomb." The angel had told them not to "be alarmed" but now "they were afraid": left speechless, saying "nothing to anyone" for the time being. It had all been too much to take in. They'd set out that morning thinking they knew what was what. But everything has been turned upside down.

Don't you think you'd have been like them? But it was so much more so for them; they'd be there with Jesus all along. They'd heard the things he'd said. And now, against their expectations, it was coming to pass before their eyes. The truth was beginning to impinge on their stunned minds.

Yes, they were afraid. The hymn 'Let all mortal flesh keep silence', speaking of the Incarnation, has the line, "And with fear and trembling stand." The women were experiencing the holy, awesome fear that grips people when they see God in action. The terrible realisation of the significance of the crucifixion; not just the death of a man, but of God's own Son, and at the hands of a people of whom they were a part. Even as we rejoice in Jesus' resurrection, we should also have that in our minds.

The Titanic struck the iceberg on Sunday 14th April 1912, a week after Easter Day. Frank Holden was a 29-year-old stoker who'd been out drinking the night before the ship was due to sail and had failed to report for duty. Someone who'd been looking for work at the dockside was recruited in his place.

After the sinking, two boards were placed outside the White Star Line's Liverpool offices: 'known to be lost' and 'known to be saved.' In error, Frank Holden was listed amongst the lost. Three days later, he arrived home, as if returning from the dead. He was often to recount that 'someone died in my place.'

The significance of Jesus' death is that he died in our place, in place of you and me; for my sin and for your sin. His bodily resurrection is the pattern for what will happen to us. All will rise from death, as he did, at the General Resurrection of the dead, at Jesus' Second Coming. Whether we are counted amongst those lost or those saved depends on our belief in Jesus.

Peter is the primary source for Mark's gospel account. He'd been brutally honest about his shortcomings, how he'd denied Jesus and "broke down and wept" [Mk. 14:72] having done so. But now he makes sure that Mark records the young man's words in full: "tell his disciples and Peter, '[Jesus] is going ahead of you into Galilee. There you will see him, just as he told you' " [v. 7].

How precious those words "and Peter" must have been to him, marking a reassurance of his forgiveness. They are an assurance to us that God's love, shown forth in Jesus, is such that our standing before him is not on the basis of what we have done or failed to do. No-one need write themselves off as 'not good enough'. We all stand before God as sinners in need of his forgiveness. And that forgiveness is freely offered, on the basis of our belief in Jesus: his death and resurrection. Alleluia! Christ is risen. He is risen indeed.

Alleluia!

Mark 16:9–20, April 3rd 2016

While I was a student at Durham in the early 1980s, I occasionally played hooky in the evening and caught the train to Newcastle, to attend the evening service at Jesmond Parish Church, having dutifully been at St. Nicholas's, Durham in the morning, you understand.

On one such occasion, the Vicar of Jesmond, David Holloway, who, interestingly, is still vicar there, told us that the home groups would be coming to the end of Rom. ch. 16. This was significant, as they'd been working through that part of the Bible for the last two years. He was referring to the whole of the Epistle to the Romans, but it didn't stop the wag sitting next to me leaning over and saying, "And that's two years just on ch. 16."

Today, likewise, is a milestone. We began our Mark preaching series in March 2014. It reached its climax last Sunday, Easter Day, with Mark's account of the Resurrection, ending at ch. 16, v. 8. Some would say that's exactly where we should have left off; believing on grounds of modern textual criticism that v. 8 marks the end of Mark's account proper.

But every translation of the Bible of which I'm aware allows, in some way, for the fact that vv. 9–20 exist in Mk. ch. 16. That includes the modern NIV, which we have in the pews here at Holy Trinity. On that basis, we are going to round off our series on Mark with ch. 16, vv. 9–20.

What do Rectors do on their day off? No doubt, strange things, as, let's face it, they're something of a race apart. As evidence of this, on Easter Monday I listened to recordings of Easter sermons friends of mine had given the day before.

First, Jacob Smith at Calvary St. George in New York. The summary given says Jacob "explores the meaning of the term 'closed,' and how the resurrection of Jesus flips this concept on its head."

Then I listened to Barry Parker at St. Paul's, Bloor Street, in Toronto. His sermon was entitled "The Funeral of Death." He started by recounting a conversation with a 'Christmas and Easter' parishioner, who wanted an answer to the "So what?" question: "So what if Jesus did rise bodily from death?"

I stand by my Easter Day offering. I think that the biblical case for Jesus' resurrection needed to be made, particularly in the face of scepticism. But there's also the need to do what Jacob and Barry did, in fleshing out the implications of Jesus' resurrection for us.

Some feel that ending Mark's account at v. 8 is entirely appropriate, ending on something of a cliff-hanger. But it doesn't really provide much basis for looking at the implications of Jesus' resurrection. That's where I hope that vv. 9-20 will prove helpful. I invite you to turn to the passage, p. 989 in the church Bibles.

I included a note on the back of Palm Sunday's order of service, about how, at first, Easter was the only Christian festival; and how it lasted for 50 days, ending on Whit Sunday, and incorporating Jesus' ascension. We know that Jesus spent the time between his resurrection and ascension, with the disciples, teaching them further; as Luke puts it: "he opened their minds so they could understand the Scriptures", Lk. 24:45. Vv. 15-18 of our Mark passage gives us part of what Jesus taught them.

V. 15: "[Jesus] said to them, 'Go into all the world and preach the good news to all creation.'" Tom Wright, my erstwhile bishop, says in his commentary: "The passage ... can prompt us to think about our own discipleship, our own commission from the risen Jesus. Would he have to chide us for our unbelief and hardheartedness? Would we be found to be preaching the gospel with as much fervour as Jesus here commands? And how, in particular, would we apply today the very interesting instruction ... to preach the gospel not just to every creature but to the entire creation?"

We are to, "Go [out] into all the world." We are not just to remain indoors, inside church, inside our homes. Yes, we can evangelise with those we already know, our families and friends; although I wonder if this mission field is one we often neglect. But there's also a need to engage with those whom God has yet to put across our path, and not to be afraid of sharing the "good news" with them.

What is the "good news"? The timing of this 'great commission' is pretty good evidence of what it consists: that Jesus not only died for our sins, but also rose from death three days later. As Paul puts it in Rom. 10:9, "If you declare with your mouth, 'Jesus is Lord,' and believe in your heart that God raised him from the dead, you will be saved."

This was new teaching from Jesus, not only because it came after practical experience of the Resurrection, but also because of its implication that it was to include Gentiles as well as Jews. During their previous ministry, Jesus and the disciples had not done this, restricting their ministry "only to the lost sheep of the house of Israel", Mt. 15:24.

J.C. Ryle writes, "The Lord Jesus would have us know that all the world needs the Gospel ... We come short of the fullness of Christ's words, and take away from the breadth of His sayings, if we shrink away from telling anyone, 'God is full of love to you, Christ is willing to save you.' "

Mission is from the Latin word meaning "send." What are we sent to do? To preach. I feel that mission is sometimes downgraded into doing good works: we must listen, understand, befriend, but we mustn't preach. Friends, as Paul puts it in Rom. 10:14, "how can they believe in the one of whom they have not heard? And how can they hear without someone preaching to them?"

Ryle wrote his commentary in 1856. I was amazed to discover that even then there were those who opposed evangelism. He rebutted such an attitude, with words stronger than I could ever use: "Let us labour on, unmoved by the sneers and taunts of those who disapprove missionary operations and hold them up to scorn. We may well pity such people. They only show their ignorance, both of Scripture and of Christ's will."

Tom Wright's comment about "all creation" ties in with Paul's teaching that "the creation itself will be liberated from its bondage to decay and brought into the glorious freedom of the children of God", Rom. 8:21; and John's vision in Revelation ch. 21 of "a new heaven and a new earth." It is this "new earth" that the redeemed will inhabit, and it is related to the present earth; we need to take good care of the planet we have been entrusted to steward.

The urgency behind the imperative to tell people about Jesus is shown in Jesus' words in v. 16 of our passage: "Whoever believes and is baptised will be saved, but whoever does not believe will be condemned." There's a clear divide between those who believe in Jesus, accepting that he died for their sins and rose again from death showing the way to eternal life; and those who do not believe and "will be condemned."

And it's not a matter of belief or baptism but belief and baptism. As Ryle puts it, baptism "is an ordinance generally necessary to salvation, where it can be had ... The baptismal water itself conveys no grace. We must look far beyond the mere outward element, to Him who commanded it to be used. But the public confession of Christ, which is implied by the use of that water, is a sacramental act, which our Master Himself has commanded; and when the ordinance is rightly used, we may confidently believe that He seals it by his blessing."

Having dealt with Gretta Vosper last Sunday, it's now time for Christopher Hitchens. Yesterday, I watched his 2008 debate with his brother Peter, whom I've met. Christopher is the atheist; Peter is the Anglican. Christopher attacked theism, describing it as "belief in a God who cares about you, knows who you are, minds what you do, answers your prayers." That is exactly the God I believe in. That is the God the Bible reveals, most specifically in Jesus Christ.

We are not left to our own devices by Jesus in evangelism as in any other matter. He is with us. He does care for us; he knows who we are, minds what we do, and answers our prayers. And in vv. 17 and 18 Jesus speaks of "signs" of his presence with believers.

Alan Cole, whom I've also met, writes in his commentary, "Every one of these evidential 'signs', except possibly the drinking of lethal draughts, was fulfilled in detail in the history of the early Church. The phenomenon of tongues, for instance, is particularly prominent from Pentecost onwards. In Acts 16:18 Paul expels a demon; in Acts 28:5 he shakes off a snake into a fire; in Acts 28:8,9 he lays his hand on many sick and heals them." A Study Bible I consulted, though, helpfully commented, "There is no command to pick up serpents or to drink deadly poison"!

Should we expect such signs nowadays? Ryle thinks not, writing, "They were never meant to continue beyond the first establishment of the Church. It is only when plants are first planted that they need daily watering and support."

Cole is more nuanced in his opinion, perhaps in the light of more recent charismatic developments in the Church. He writes: "Whether or no such evidential manifestations were intended to be continuous in the life of the Church, or restricted to this period, or sporadic, must be considered in the light of the rest of the New Testament."

I wish to conclude by pointing out the delightful symmetry of the passage. Jesus told the disciples in v. 15, "Go into all the world and preach the good news to all creation." V. 20 records how they responded to Jesus' command: "the disciples went out and preached everywhere, and the Lord worked with them and confirmed his word by the signs that accompanied it." They did as Jesus commanded them to do.

As Jesus says in Lk. 11:28, "Blessed ... are those who hear the word of God and obey it." May we, as Jesus' disciples, likewise follow the example of the Eleven.

Amen.

O ALMIGHTY God, who hast instructed thy holy Church with the heavenly doctrine of thy Evangelist Saint Mark: Give us grace, that, being not like children carried away with every blast of vain doctrine, we may be established in the truth of thy holy Gospel; through Jesus Christ our Lord.

Amen.

[i] From C.S. Lewis, *The Lion, the Witch & The Wardrobe* Chapter 7 (Penguin, 1950).
[ii] https://www.theglobeandmail.com/opinion/marriage-is-the-new-class-divide/article23545818/

www.ingramcontent.com/pod-product-compliance
Lightning Source LLC
Chambersburg PA
CBHW072149100526
44589CB00015B/2147